Cooking Up
COMFORT

100 Simple, Soothing Recipes

Cooking Up
COMFORT

100 Simple, Soothing Recipes

Althea McQuestion

■ WILLOW CREEK PRESS®

Published by Willow Creek Press
P.O. Box 147, Minocqua, Wisconsin 54548

For information on other Willow Creek Press titles,
call 1-800-850-9453

Printed in Canada

Contents

Introduction

COOKING HAS ALWAYS BEEN A PASSION OF MINE. GROWING UP IN A LARGE ITALIAN-IRISH FAMILY with four other siblings plus mom and dad, food has always been a big and important part of all our lives. Everyone helped in the kitchen and participated with finding new and creative ways to prepare fresh dishes while keeping it simple, practical, within a budget and most of all, fun—because to me, that's what it is all about. Cooking and being in the kitchen should be all about fun, laughter and togetherness. Some of the best memories are the ones spent with my family in the kitchen—my favorite was birthdays. As a treat on this special day, my mom would prepare our favorite requested dish—which for me was always either lasagna or Swedish meatballs—but what I looked most forward to was the cake, since we would bake it together. At the same time, the birthday girl or boy was given the freedom to decorate it on their own, and in any way they desire. We could lather on as much icing as we wanted, or smother it with so many candies that you couldn't even see the frosting, and it didn't matter, because it was "your day" and you could do what made you happy. Being together in the kitchen with mom and just being able to have that alone time—baking, laughing, creating—just made me feel so special. I'll never forget moments like that and hope to one day continue them with children of my own.

For me, how it all started was with baking. I love to bake breads, pastries, pies and cookies, but my absolute favorite is baking and decorating cakes. I love to let my imagination soar and design something that is different, colorful and representative of the one receiving it. At the age of 15, I was out on my own to take on the world and began working at a bakery—and loved it. Every day after school, I would work as many hours as possible and became hooked. I remained in school, went on to college and graduated with a diploma in Medical Health and Science. Throughout college and before I graduated and began working in a regional hospital with the Diagnostic Imaging/Cardiology Department, I worked in a family operated and owned restaurant. I mostly waitressed but showed enthusiasm for the kitchen and began helping with food preparation. Soon after, I became more interested with cooking and food presentation. Although I've always known how to cook, with a large amount of my skill having been self-taught or obtained through hands-on experience from being in the kitchen with my family, working in the restaurant really opened up my senses. It gave me a passion for food but even more so, a passion to create really good food. I used to love peeking out of the kitchen just to see the people's expressions or reactions after eating something that I had made; it was something that always gave me such great satisfaction and pride.

In this book, some of the recipes are family loved and have been enjoyed enormously throughout my life. Some were handed down from my mother and some came from ideas, but most came from the heart, because that's how I learned to cook and that's how I still cook today. I believe and always find that even with the simplest of foods and ingredients, a dish can still turn out to be great just by putting your heart and a little imagination into it.

Simply knowing flavors and the combinations of them, can give you the power and ability to invent or create anything without ever having to open a book. Now don't get me wrong, cookbooks are extremely helpful and resourceful, but have you ever noticed that sometimes you just whip up something using items found in the pantry or fridge and it turns out amazing?!? Usually, something that was just created on a whim and with limited ingredients, and the next thing you know, your adding a bit of this and a little of that, or thinking ooh, what about those and in the end you've got something fabulous—that's what I'm talking about.

I wanted to write this book for many reasons. It's not just about food and recipes, but the cherished moments that go with them. When cooking, you're not just creating food; you're creating and capturing the memories from all the moments that were shared during this ritual.

Let's face it, most events and socials largely revolve around food. Whether it be preparing, serving or enjoying. It's something we all need, something we all love, and something to this day that can still bring family and friends together. Certain dishes will remind me of places I've journeyed or a special someone. Certain smells and aromas will trigger a memory of an event or time. In any case, it's all special and unique to the individual. Later in this book (page 114), I share a favorite memory of mine called "pancake Sundays with Dad". Even now to this day, every time I make pancakes with my family, I remember my dad and all the fun we shared. I also wrote this book because I wanted a way to display both my recipes and family favorites—for myself, for my readers and hopefully one day, for my children.

Some of these recipes are from family, which we have prepared or enjoyed most of our lives. Some were stumbled upon, and have now made their way onto our table, and some were given by friends. But most of the recipes are created with passion and from the heart, which is why comfort on a plate is the best way to describe many of dishes that you will be creating and enjoying from this collection. 100 of my favorite deliciously comforting and soul soothing recipes to look forward to at each and every meal—which is something that many of us need and crave, especially in today's world.

The best advice I can give anyone in relation to cooking, is to have fun. It doesn't have to be perfect and there's nothing that can't be undone, so just jump in and get into it with no reservation or hesitation. Cooking should never be intimidating or considered a chore. Look at it as time together or as a time to relax when creating alone. Cooking can be very therapeutic. So jump in, have fun, get dirty, make a mess, create, explore and laugh but importantly, enjoy.

I hope you enjoy exploring this book as much as I did writing and putting it together. I hope you enjoy the traditions that I've grown up with and that are largely responsible for implanting the seed in me that has grown into such a passion. Cook, share, laugh and enjoy but most of all love and have fun.

From my heart to your table
Sincerely,

Althea McQuestion

Sides & Accompaniments

Roasted Asparagus Wrapped in Prosciutto Serves 4

PROSCIUTTO IS SO VERSATILE; IT CAN BE USED WITH VARIOUS FOODS AND IN VARIOUS WAYS. For this side dish, I just wrapped thin slices of prosciutto around asparagus and roast them for a short time.

- · 12 asparagus stalks, trimmed
- · 1 tablespoon olive oil
- · ½ teaspoon salt
- · 1 teaspoon black pepper

- · 1 tablespoon grated Parmesan cheese
- · 12 slices prosciutto, paper thin

1. Preheat oven to 450°F.

2. Toss the asparagus with the olive oil, salt and pepper. Wrap each piece of asparagus with one slice of prosciutto leaving the tips of asparagus exposed. Place on baking sheet and cook for 15 minutes. Remove from oven and let cool.

3. Arrange asparagus on a serving platter and sprinkle with Parmesan cheese.

Beer Glazed Vegetables

Serves 2

VEGETABLES NEVER HAD IT SO GOOD. YOUR FAMILY MAY LIKE THEIR VEGETABLES, BUT when prepared this way, they'll LOVE their vegetables. This is best served over mashed potatoes alongside chicken or steak.

- 1 tablespoon butter plus 1 teaspoon, divided
- 1 large red onion, finely chopped
- 3 garlic cloves, finely sliced
- 2 carrots, peeled and cut into ½-inch pieces
- 2 parsnips, peeled and cut into ½-inch pieces
- ½ cup sliced cremini mushrooms
- 2 celery stalks, cut into ½-inch pieces
- 1 teaspoon sugar
- 1 teaspoon fresh thyme leaves
- 1 bottle (12 oz.) of your favorite beer
- salt and pepper to taste

1. In a medium saucepan over medium heat, melt 1 tablespoon of butter. Add the onion and sauté for 4 minutes, then add the garlic and sauté for 2 minutes longer. Add the carrots, parsnips, mushrooms, celery, sugar and thyme. Mix together and season with salt and pepper to coat.

2. Add beer (enough to cover vegetables—you may need a second bottle), cover and bring to a boil. Reduce heat and allow to simmer uncovered, until most of the liquid has evaporated and vegetables are tender (approximately 20-25 minutes). If all liquid has evaporated before vegetables are finished, add a little more beer and continue to simmer.

3. When liquid has reduced to approximately ½ cup, add a teaspoon of butter and shake pan to coat vegetables with glaze and make gravy. Season with salt and pepper. Serve over mashed potatoes or rice.

Potato and Shiitake Mushroom Gratin with Asiago cheese

Serves 6

A GRATIN LAYERED WITH ASIAGO CHEESE, SHIITAKE MUSHROOMS AND POTATOES. THIS DOES take a little time to prepare and assemble, but the final result makes slicing all those potatoes worth it.

- **6 tablespoons butter**
- **3 pounds fresh shiitake mushrooms, stemmed and thinly sliced**
- **3 garlic cloves, minced**
- **2 teaspoons thyme**
- **1 teaspoon rosemary**

- **1 teaspoon salt and pepper**
- **3 pounds baking potatoes, washed and very thinly sliced**
- **1 cup Parmesan cheese**
- **1 cup asiago cheese**
- **2 cups heavy cream**
- **2 cups half-and-half**

1. Preheat oven to 375°F.

2. In a large pot over high heat, add the butter and mushrooms and sauté until liquid evaporates (approximately 8-10 minutes). Add the garlic, thyme and rosemary and continue to sauté for 1 minute. In a saucepan over medium-low heat, add the cream and half-and-half. Heat until just under a boil then remove from heat, cover and set aside.

3. Lightly butter a deep ovenproof casserole dish, arrange ⅓ of the potatoes, overlapping slightly. Top the potatoes with half of the mushroom mixture and sprinkle ⅓ of the asiago and Parmesan cheese over the mushrooms. Repeat layering ⅓ of the potatoes, remaining mushroom mixture and remaining asiago and Parmesan cheese. Arrange the remaining potatoes atop the cheese and using a spatula, press the layers down to condense. Pour the cream over the top, sprinkle with a little more salt and pepper (top with a little more asiago cheese if desired). Cover loosely with foil and bake for 1 hour until the potatoes are tender. Uncover and bake for an additional 15 minutes until the cheese melts and the edges are golden. Let stand for 8-10 minutes before serving.

Stuffed Tomatoes with Wild Rice and Parmesan Cheese

TOMATOES FILLED WITH WILD RICE, WALNUTS AND PARMESAN CHEESE.

- · 6 medium sized tomatoes
- · 1 teaspoon salt
- · 1 teaspoon black pepper
- · ¾ cup (6 oz.) long-grain wild rice mix

- · 3 tablespoons grated Parmesan cheese
- · 2 tablespoons olive oil
- · 2 ounces chopped walnuts

1. Preheat oven to 375°F.

2. Slice the top off of each tomato (reserve tops and return to stuffed tomatoes before baking if desired) and scoop out the pulp from the center and reserve for later. Season the tomato cavities with salt and pepper.

3. Prepare the rice according to the directions on the package. Drain rice and transfer to a bowl. Stir in the Parmesan cheese, ½ cup of the reserved pulp and walnuts until well blended. Spoon the pilaf into tomatoes, slightly mounding. Arrange stuffed tomatoes, sides touching in a small baking dish. Drizzle each with olive oil and sprinkle with a little extra Parmesan cheese if desired (replace the reserved tops).

4. Bake for 25 minutes or until tomatoes are tender and the rice is heated through.

Orzo with Tomatoes, Garbanzo Beans and Goat Cheese

Serves 6

OKAY, I KNOW ORZO IS PASTA BUT I ADDED THIS RECIPE IN THE CHAPTER FOR SIDE DISHES because it makes a nice accompaniment for an entrée. You can also substitute the Orzo for rice if needed. This is great when served at room temperature and tastes even better the next day when the flavors have married. If you don't like goat cheese just substitute with crumbled feta.

- 1½ cups (9 oz.) orzo
- 1 can (15 oz.) garbanzo beans "chickpeas", drained and rinsed
- 1½ cups grape tomatoes, halved
- 3 tablespoons lemon juice
- ½ cup fresh basil, chopped
- 1 cup (15 oz.) soft fresh goat cheese, crumbed
- 2 tablespoon balsamic vinaigrette
- 1 teaspoon oregano
- salt and pepper

1. In a large pot of lightly salted boiling water, add the orzo. Cover partially and cook, stirring frequently until the orzo is al dente (approximately 7 minutes). Drain the orzo and transfer to a large bowl. Set aside and allow the orzo to cool completely.

2. Toss the orzo with the beans, tomatoes, basil, vinaigrette, oregano and lemon juice. Mix in the cheese and season with salt and pepper to taste. Serve at room temperature.

Brussels Sprouts with Pancetta Thyme and Sage · Serves 6

BRUSSELS SPROUTS ARE ONE OF MY FAVORITE VEGETABLES AND I EAT THEM OFTEN. IF you're not a big fan of this vegetable, you will be after you taste this. Brussels sprouts mixed with pancetta, garlic, thyme and sage. This will certainly awaken your taste buds.

- **2 tablespoons olive oil**
- **6 ounces pancetta diced into ¼-inch pieces**
- **1½ pounds brussels sprouts, trimmed and halved**
- **1 small onion, diced**
- **¾ teaspoon salt and pepper**

- **1¾ cups of chicken broth**
- **1 teaspoon thyme**
- **1 teaspoon sage**
- **2 garlic cloves, minced**
- **2 tablespoons slivered almonds, blanched**

1. In a large saucepan over medium heat, add the oil and pancetta. Cook the pancetta, stirring often until golden brown, crisp and fat has rendered (approximately 5-8 minutes). With a slotted spoon remove the pancetta to a plate and set aside.

2. In the same saucepan over medium heat, add the brussels sprouts, onion, garlic, salt, pepper, thyme and sage. Sauté for 5 minutes or until the brussels sprouts are lightly browned. Add the chicken broth and lower the heat. Cook, stirring occasionally until the sprouts are fork tender (approximately 15 minutes). If the pan becomes a little dry, add a little more broth or water. Return the pancetta to the pan and heat through. Transfer to serving dish, sprinkle with the almonds and enjoy.

Baked Mashed Potatoes with Basil Pesto and a Parmesan Topping

Serves 4-6

CREAMY MASHED POTATOES, TOPPED WITH A LIGHT BREAD CRUMB AND PARMESAN cheese coating.

- 1 tablespoon butter, for greasing dish
- 4 pounds russet potatoes peeled and cut into pieces
- 1 cup milk
- ½ cup butter (1 stick)
- 2 tablespoons basil pesto
- 1 cup shredded mozzarella cheese

- ½ cup shredded cheddar cheese
- 1 cup grated Parmesan cheese
- 1 teaspoon black pepper
- ½ teaspoon salt
- ¼ cup dried plain bread crumbs

1. Preheat oven to 400°F.

2. Coat a 13x9-inch casserole dish with the 1 tablespoon of butter. Set aside.

3. In a large pot of salted boiling water, cook the potatoes until they are tender (approximately 15 minutes). Drain well and return potatoes to the same pot and mash well. Beat in the milk, butter, pesto, mozzarella cheese, cheddar cheese and ¾ cup of the Parmesan cheese. Season with salt and pepper.

4. Pour mashed potatoes into the prepared casserole dish. In a small bowl, mix together the bread crumbs and the remaining Parmesan cheese. Sprinkle the breadcrumb mixture evenly over the top of the mashed potatoes. Bake uncovered for 20 minutes or until the top is golden brown.

Creamy Lemon Rice

THIS FRAGRANT AND CREAMY RICE DISH IS FLAVORED USING LEMON ZEST AND LEMON JUICE mixed into the rice with sour cream. This is a perfect accompaniment for chicken or fish.

- 1 cup Arborio rice
- 2 tablespoons butter
- 1 teaspoon grated lemon rind
- 1¾ cups water, boiling hot
- ½ teaspoon salt

- 1 tablespoon lemon juice
- ¾ cup sour cream
- 1 teaspoon black pepper
- 2 tablespoons fresh parsley, chopped (for garnish)

1. In a saucepan, melt the butter. Stir in the rice and lemon rind and cook over moderate heat, stirring until rice is opaque (approximately 5 minutes). Stir in boiling water and salt. Cover. Simmer until rice is tender and liquid has absorbed (approximately 20-25 minutes).

2. Stir in lemon juice and sour cream. Cook over low heat until just heated through. Season with pepper and transfer to a serving dish. Garnish with parsley and grated lemon rind if desired.

Cauliflower Gratin with Swiss Cheese

A VEGETABLE GRATIN IS AN EXCELLENT CHOICE TO BRING TO A POTLUCK OR PICNIC. THEY are simple to make, can feed a crowd and can be made ahead of time. This gratin is an easy, cheesy and delicious way to eat your vegetables.

- 1 large head of cauliflower, cut into florets
- 4 tablespoons unsalted butter, divided
- 3 tablespoons all-purpose flour
- 2 cups heavy cream, hot
- ¼ teaspoon grated nutmeg

- ½ teaspoon salt
- ½ teaspoon black pepper
- ¾ cup grated Swiss cheese, divided
- ½ cup grated Parmesan cheese
- ¼ cup bread crumbs

1. Preheat oven to 375°F.

2. In a large pot of lightly salted boiling water, add the cauliflower florets. Boil until tender but still firm (approximately 5-6 minutes). Drain and set aside.

3. In a medium saucepan over low heat, melt 2 tablespoons of butter. Add the flour, stirring constantly for 2 minutes. Pour the hot cream into the butter flour mixture. Whisk constantly until it comes to a boil and thickens (approximately 1 minute). Remove mixture from heat and add the nutmeg, salt, pepper and ½ cup of the Swiss and Parmesan cheese.

4. In a deep 8x11-inch baking dish, pour in ⅓ cup of the sauce along the bottom. Transfer the cauliflower into the baking dish and spoon the rest of the sauce evenly on top of the cauliflower. Sprinkle the top with the remaining Swiss cheese and the bread crumbs. Dot the top with the remaining 2 tablespoons of butter. Bake for 25-30 minutes or until the top is nicely browned.

Maple Glazed Acorn Squash

Makes 4 Servings

HERE'S ANOTHER RECIPE THAT I LOVE TO PREPARE AND THINK OF MY DAD EVERY TIME. He loved acorn squash and always made it this way. If we were out of syrup, he would use brown sugar. Both are good.

- 1 large acorn or golden acorn squash
- ½ cup water
- 3 tablespoons pure maple syrup

- 2 teaspoons clover honey
- 1 tablespoon butter, melted
- ¼ teaspoon cinnamon

1. Preheat oven to 375°F.

2. Remove the blossom ends and stems from squash. Cut squash crosswise into four equal parts. Using a large spoon, discard seeds and membrane.

3. Pour the water into a 13x9-inch baking dish and add the squash. Cover with foil and bake for 30 minutes or until fork tender.

4. In a small bowl, combine the syrup, honey, butter and cinnamon. Remove the squash from the oven and pour off the water. Brush the syrup mixture over the squash, coating completely. Pour any remaining sauce into the dish with squash. Return to oven and bake uncovered for 10 minutes or until syrup is bubbling. Cool slightly and eat.

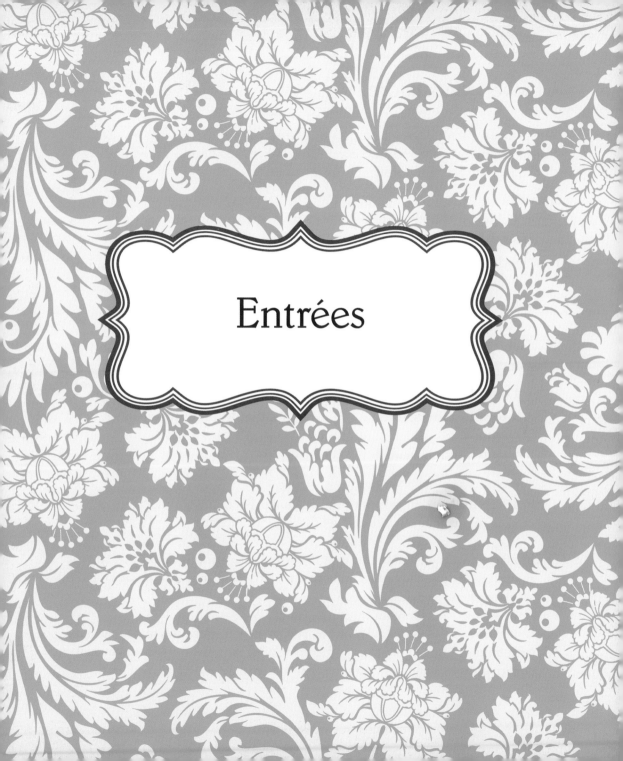

Entrées

Chicken Cacciatore

Serves 6

THIS IS A GREAT CACCIATORE RECIPE. THE SAUCE IS NOT THE THICK, RICH, FATTY KIND that is customary to chicken cacciatore. This is a light and healthier modification that will deliver the same satisfying taste, but with less fat.

- **4 chicken breasts (skin on, bone in)**
- **2 chicken thighs (skin on)**
- **½ cup all-purpose flour**
- **½ red bell pepper, chopped**
- **½ yellow bell pepper, chopped**
- **½ green bell pepper, chopped**
- **1 onion, finely chopped**
- **5-6 garlic cloves, finely chopped**
- **3 tablespoons olive oil**

- **1 teaspoon salt**
- **1 teaspoon black pepper**
- **1 tablespoon Italian seasoning**
- **¾ cup dry white wine**
- **1 can (28 ounces) diced tomatoes with juice**
- **¾ cup chicken broth**
- **2 tablespoons chopped fresh parsley**
- **1 tablespoon chopped fresh basil**

1. In a deep shallow dish, add the flour, salt and pepper. Dredge each piece of chicken in the flour mixture and lightly coat. Set aside.

2. In a large saucepan, heat the oil over medium heat. Working in batches, add the chicken to the pan and brown on both sides (approximately 4-5 minutes). Do this for all chicken pieces and set aside.

3. Using the same saucepan, add the bell pepper, onion, garlic and seasoning. Sauté for 5 minutes. Add in the wine and simmer until the wine has reduced by half (approximately 3 minutes). Add the tomatoes with juice and chicken broth.

4. Return the chicken to the pan, turning pieces to coat. Cover and simmer over medium-low heat until the chicken is cooked (approximately 25-30 minutes depending on pieces).

5. Remove the cooked chicken from the pan and plate on a large serving platter. Boil the sauce until it thickens (approximately 3-4 minutes), removing any excess fat from atop the sauce. Spoon sauce over the chicken and sprinkle with chopped parsley and basil. Serve.

Stuffed Chicken with Apples, Walnuts and Raisins Serves 6

STUFFING POULTRY OR PORK WITH FRUIT ADDS A NICE LIGHT SWEET TASTE TO THE MEAT. I like to use apples, pears, raisins, cranberries and peache—just to name a few favorites.

- **6 boneless, skinless chicken breasts**
- **2 medium red delicious apples, finely chopped**
- **1 cup golden or dark raisins**
- **1 cup chopped walnuts**
- **1½ cups wild rice**

- **1 cup feta cheese**
- **1 tablespoon black pepper**
- **2 teaspoon salt**
- **5 tablespoons vegetable oil**
- **6 rosemary sprigs**

1. Preheat oven to 350°F.

2. In a medium pot of lightly salted water, add the rice and boil until tender, (approximately 12-15 minutes). Drain and set aside.

3. Butterfly the chicken breasts and lightly pound using a meat mallet between parchment paper to slightly flatten. Drizzle the chicken cutlets using 3 tablespoons of the olive oil. Sprinkle with salt and pepper

4. In a large bowl, mix the chopped apples, walnuts, raisins, cooked rice and feta. Spoon generous amounts of mixture into the center of each chicken breast. Fold over and tuck in ends to seal in the stuffing. Place stuffed chicken breasts on a large baking sheet and drizzle the remaining oil over top of each breast. Season with a little more salt and pepper and place a rosemary sprig on the top of each stuffed chicken breast. Bake for 30-35 minutes.

Prosciutto Wrapped Chicken with Blue Cheese and Pecans

Serves 4

TENDER CHICKEN FILLED WITH BLUE CHEESE AND PECANS WRAPPED IN A BLANKET OF PROSCIUTTO.

- **4 boneless, skinless chicken breasts**
- **1 cup blue cheese, crumbled**
- **½ cup pecans, chopped**

- **8 thin slices smoked prosciutto**
- **salt and pepper**
- **olive oil**

1. Butterfly the chicken breasts and pound lightly between parchment paper, using a meat mallet to slightly flatten. Drizzle each chicken cutlet with a small amount of olive oil then sprinkle with salt and pepper to season. Spoon generous amounts of the cheese and pecans into the center of the chicken. Fold over and tuck in ends to seal in stuffing. Wrap each stuffed chicken breast with 2 slices of prosciutto and place on a baking sheet. Bake for 30-35 minutes.

Maple Syrup & Beer Braised Pork Butt Serves 6

THIS SLOWLY BRAISED PORK BUTT IS JUICY, TENDER AND FULL OF MELT-IN-YOUR-MOUTH goodness. This is great for a dinner party because it can be prepared ahead of time and tossed in the oven before your guests arrive. The only thing that will be left to do is sit and enjoy.

- **6 pounds boneless pork butt roast**
- **¼ cup paprika**
- **2 tablespoons black pepper**
- **½ teaspoon sage**
- **½ teaspoon thyme**

- **1 tablespoon garlic powder**
- **1 teaspoon salt**
- **3 cups light beer**
- **1 cup maple syrup**
- **8 garlic cloves, minced**

1. Preheat oven to 500°F.

2. In a small bowl, combine the paprika, black pepper, sage, thyme, garlic powder and salt. Rub mixture on the pork butt, pressing onto the surface and coating it evenly. Place seasoned meat on a roasting rack in a roasting pan. Roast in the oven for 15 minutes (this will give the surface of the meat a nice brown color). Remove the roast and reduce oven temperature to 250°F. Carefully transfer pork butt from roasting pan to a large oven-proof casserole dish or Dutch oven.

3. In a separate medium bowl, mix the beer and maple syrup until well combined. Pour the mixture over the pork and add the whole garlic cloves to dish. Cover and cook in the oven for 2 hours or until the meat is tender and soft to the touch. Remove from oven and let stand for 10 minutes before cutting. Serve with mashed potatoes and vegetables.

Turkey Tournedos

- turkey tenderloin
- 6 strips bacon
- 1 can cranberry sauce, warmed
- 2 tablespoons vegetable oil
- salt and pepper

1. Have your butcher cut the turkey tenderloin into 2 inch thick parts. Brush tenderloins with vegetable oil and season sides with salt and pepper. Wrap each tenderloin with one strip of bacon and place on baking sheet. Bake in oven at 350°F for 20–25 minutes, turning halfway between cook time. Remove from oven and transfer to serving plate. Spoon warm cranberry sauce over the tenderloins and serve.

Italian Stuffed Chicken

Serves 4

CHICKEN BREAST STUFFED WITH ROASTED RED PEPPERS, SPINACH, MOZZARELLA CHEESE with a Parmesan seasoned dressing.

- 4 boneless, skinless chicken breasts
- 1 tablespoon Italian seasoning
- 2 tablespoons grated Parmesan cheese
- ¾ cup jarred roasted red peppers, drained and sliced
- ¼ cup fresh spinach, chopped
- 4 tablespoons shredded mozzarella cheese
- ¼ cup zesty Italian dressing
- salt and pepper
- olive oil

1. Preheat oven to 350°F.

2. Butterfly the chicken breasts and lightly pound using a meat mallet between parchment paper to slightly flatten. Sprinkle each cutlet with salt and pepper.

3. In a small bowl, combine the Italian dressing, Parmesan cheese and seasoning. Spoon mixture into the center of each chicken cutlet. Place a little of the chopped spinach followed by three strips of red pepper over top of the Parmesan mixture. Sprinkle each cutlet with 1 tablespoon of mozzarella cheese and roll each breast up. Place on a nonstick baking sheet and lightly drizzle each with olive oil. Bake for 30-35 minutes.

Crown Pork Roast with Wild Rice

Serves 8

THIS MAGNIFICENT DISPLAY NOT ONLY LOOKS IMPRESSIVE BUT TASTES OUT OF THIS WORLD. Crown roast of pork stuffed with wild rice, dried fruit and nuts. Serve this for the next dinner party; your guests will surely be satisfied.

- 8 pound crown pork roast
- salt and pepper for seasoning
- 1 pound wild rice
- 10 cups water
- 2 shallots, minced
- ½ cup dried cranberries
- 1 cup slivered dried pears
- 1 teaspoon minced fresh rosemary
- 1 cup walnuts, coarsely chopped
- ½ teaspoon red wine vinegar

1. Preheat the oven to 300°F.

2. Season the roast generously with salt and pepper. Place roast upside down in a large roasting pan so it is supported by the rib bones. Roast in oven for 30 minutes. Turn meat over and continue cooking, uncovered for 2 hours or until internal temperature of 140°F.

3. Meanwhile, in a large saucepan over medium-high heat, combine the water, ½ teaspoon of salt and the rice. Cook rice, uncovered, for 45 minutes or until tender. Drain and return rice to the saucepan. Add the shallots, cranberries, pears and rosemary. Cover the pan and let stand at room temperature until the roast is done.

4. When roast is ready, add the walnuts and red wine vinegar to the rice mix and stir. Season with salt and pepper to taste. Spoon as much of the rice filling as possible into the center of the crown roast. Spoon some of the fat from the bottom of roasting pan over the stuffing. Return the meat to the oven (place the remaining rice stuffing in a baking dish and keep aside) and cook the roast for an additional 10-15 minutes or until internal temperature of 145°F. Remove from oven and let stand for 10 minutes. Transfer crown roast to serving plate and spoon the additional rice mixture from the baking dish around the roast. Serve.

Herb-Roasted Rack of Lamb

Serves 4

I REALLY LIKE LAMB AND THE RACK OF LAMB IS MY FAVORITE CUT—I THINK IT TASTES A little less gamey than some of the others. I Prepare it using a pesto made with basil, rosemary, thyme and garlic. This adds moistness to the lamb as well as an enhanced flavor. Have your butcher French the lamb (clean out between the bones). A clean bone will make the presentation better and easier for your guests to pick up and eat.

- ½ cup lightly packed fresh basil leaves
- ½ cup lightly packed fresh thyme leaves
- 1 tablespoon fresh rosemary leaves, lightly chopped
- 1 tablespoon freshly grated Parmesan cheese
- 1 tablespoon lemon juice
- 2 garlic cloves
- ½ teaspoon salt and pepper
- 2 tablespoons olive oil
- 2 racks of lamb (approximately 1½ pounds each), Frenched

1. Using a food processor, blend the basil leaves, thyme leaves, rosemary, Parmesan, lemon juice, garlic, salt and pepper, until finely chopped. Gradually add the olive oil and blend until mixture is smooth and creamy.

2. Place the lamb into a large roasting pan (meat side up, bones curved downward) and generously brush the herb sauce mixture over the lamb coating both sides. Allow the lamb to sit at room temperature for at least 1 hour to absorb flavors (this will make the lamb very moist and succulent).

3. Preheat oven to 425°F.

4. Bake lamb for 20-25 minutes for medium-rare. Remove from the oven and allow the lamb to rest for at least 10 minutes before slicing.

Roasted Lemon Chicken with Rosemary Serves 4

ROASTING A CHICKEN WITH VEGETABLES COULDN'T BE SIMPLER OR MORE GRATIFYING. You have a moist, golden bird and savory accompaniments and it's all done in one pan. What could be easier than that! I used a small chicken for this recipe, but if you are having a crowd over for dinner just double the ingredients and pick up an extra chicken. Roasting two smaller chickens will take less time to cook than one large bird.

- 1 (4–5 pound) roasting chicken, giblets removed, cleaned and dried
- ½ teaspoon salt
- 1 teaspoon pepper
- 3 lemons, cut into quarters
- ½ navel orange, cut into wedges
- 4 fresh rosemary sprigs
- 2 medium yellow onions, peeled and cut into wedges

- 2 tablespoons olive oil
- 20 small new potatoes, halved and quartered
- 4 large carrots, cut into ½-inch pieces
- 4 garlic cloves, peeled and smashed
- 3 parsnips, cut into ½-inch pieces
- 3 tablespoons unsalted butter, melted

1. Preheat the oven to 425°F.

2. Sprinkle the chicken cavity with salt and pepper. Place the lemons, oranges and rosemary inside the cavity of the chicken. Using twine, tie the legs of the chicken together, tucking the wing tips under the body of the chicken.

3. In a roasting pan, toss the onions, potatoes, carrots, garlic and parsnips with 2 tablespoons of olive oil. Place the chicken in the roasting pan with the vegetables and brush with melted butter. Sprinkle with salt and pepper.

4. Roast for 30 minutes. Remove from oven and stir vegetables surrounding chicken. Return to oven and cook for 30-40 minutes or until juices run clear when fork is inserted into the meat near the thigh joint. Remove the chicken from the pan and tent with foil. Allow the chicken to sit for 10 minutes before carving. Toss the vegetables in the pan and transfer to a serving platter along with some of the juices. Carve the chicken and place pieces on the platter along with the vegetables.

Saucy Swedish Meatballs

Serves 6

THIS IS MY MOM'S RECIPE AND ONE OF MY FAVORITES. FOR MY BIRTHDAY, SHE WOULD always ask me what I want, and I always said the same thing—Swedish meatballs. I like to eat this over a bed of white rice.

- 2 lbs ground beef
- 2 eggs
- ¼ cup water
- 1 cup bread crumbs
- 1 small onion, finely chopped
- 1½ teaspoons salt
- 1½ teaspoons pepper

- 2 tablespoons olive oil
- 1 can (12 oz.) cranberry sauce
- 1 bottle (12 oz.) chili sauce
- 2 tablespoons brown sugar
- 1 tablespoon lemon juice

1. In a large bowl, combine the ground beef, eggs, water, bread crumbs, onion, salt and pepper. Mix together using a wooden spoon or your hands until well blended. Form into small balls.

2. In a large saucepan, heat 2 tablespoons of olive oil. Add the meatballs, turning every so often to brown on all sides. Remove from heat.

3. Using a separate large deep saucepan over medium-low heat, mix the cranberry sauce, chili sauce, brown sugar and lemon juice. Let simmer covered, until sauce is smooth. Add the cooked meatballs and simmer covered, for one hour. Serve over a bed of white rice. Enjoy.

Thanks Mom!!

Apricot Glazed Ham

Serves 6

MY BROTHER IS NOT A FAN OF HAM—HE'LL EAT IT BUT DOESN'T CARE FOR IT. HE CAME over for dinner one night, and I prepared this apricot glazed ham just for him to try. It's not all that fancy but he really liked it, and will only eat ham if it is prepared this way.

- 2-3 tablespoons butter
- ½ cup dry red wine
- ½ cup apricot jam
- 10 dried apricots, thinly sliced
- ½ teaspoon salt

- 1 teaspoon pepper
- 6 thick slices of smoked ham
- 2 tablespoons chopped fresh parsley

1. Preheat oven to 325°F.

2. Using a small ovenproof skillet or casserole dish over low heat, melt the butter. Add the red wine, jam, sliced apricots, salt and pepper. Stir until sauce is smooth.

3. Add the smoked ham slices to the dish and spoon sauce over the ham. Cover and bake for 30-35 minutes. Transfer glazed ham to a serving platter and spoon sauce overtop. Sprinkle with chopped parsley and serve. Do not overcook.

Peppered Sherried Chicken

Serves 8

- **8 boneless, skinless chicken breasts**
- **4 tablespoons black peppercorns, ground**
- **4 tablespoons olive oil**
- **½ cup dry sherry**
- **½ cup chicken broth**
- **½ teaspoon oregano**
- **½ teaspoon tarragon**
- **1 cup heavy whipping cream**
- **salt**

1. Sprinkle both sides of the chicken with peppercorns pressing them firmly into the meat. In a medium saucepan over medium heat, add the oil and cook the chicken for 6–8 minutes per side or until juices run clear. Remove chicken from pan to serving platter and tent with foil to keep warm. Set aside.

2. Drain out the excess fat from the pan and add the sherry, broth, oregano and tarragon. Bring to a rapid boil until the liquid has reduced by half. Stir in the cream until slightly thickened. Add salt to taste. Spoon sauce over the chicken and serve.

Spicy Lamb

Serves 4

THIS SPICY LAMB DISH IS MADE WITH TABASCO SAUCE, CURRY POWDER AND TOMATOES.
It's spicy but not overpowering and the yogurt topping gives it a creamy coolness.
This is great served over a bed of rice.

- 2 pounds lamb stew meat
- 4 tablespoons vegetable oil
- 2 onions, finely chopped
- 4 garlic cloves, minced
- 2 tablespoons curry powder
- ¼ teaspoon paprika
- 1 teaspoon ground cloves
- 2 tablespoons tomato paste
- 2 teaspoons Tabasco sauce
- 2 (14 oz.) cans chopped tomatoes with juice
- 3 cups chicken broth
- ½ cup grated unsweetened coconut
- ½ red bell pepper, chopped
- 1½ cups plain yogurt
- 1 tablespoon chopped fresh Italian parsley
- ½ teaspoon salt and pepper

1. In a large saucepan over medium heat, brown the meat working in small batches. Place cooked portions on a large plate and set aside.

2. In the same saucepan, add the onion, garlic, curry powder, paprika and cloves. Cook for 1 minute. Add the tomato paste, Tabasco sauce, tomatoes and their juice, broth and coconut and bring to a boil. Return the lamb back to the pan, cover and simmer for 1 hour. Add the chopped pepper and cook for an additional 10 minutes. Transfer lamb to a serving dish and season with salt and pepper. Spoon yogurt over top of the lamb and sprinkle with chopped parsley. Serve with white rice.

Veal Scaloppini with Vermouth and Wild Mushrooms

THIS IS SO GOOD AND A DEFINITE MUST IF YOU WANT TO WOW YOUR DINNER GUESTS.

- 6 veal scaloppini
- 1 cup all-purpose flour
- 1 teaspoon parsley
- 1 teaspoon thyme
- 1 teaspoon sage
- 3 tablespoons olive oil
- 1 cup wild mushrooms (such as shiitake, cremini, portabella)

- 2 teaspoons minced garlic
- ½ teaspoon salt and pepper
- ½ cup of dry vermouth (can substitute with dry white wine if needed)
- 1 cup chicken broth
- 1 cup heavy cream
- fresh chopped Italian parsley for garnish

1. In a shallow bowl or large plate, combine the flour, parsley and ½ teaspoon each of the thyme and sage. Dredge the pieces of veal in the flour mixture, coating both sides. Shake off excess and transfer to a plate. Set aside.

2. In a large saucepan over high heat, add 1 tablespoon of oil. Working in batches, add veal to the pan and brown on both sides (approximately 1-2 minutes per side). Remove from pan and set aside.

3. Using the same pan over medium-high heat, add 2 tablespoons of oil and sauté mushrooms for about 2 minutes. Add the garlic, salt and pepper and sauté for 1 minute. Add the vermouth and cook for 1 minute to reduce liquid. Add the chicken broth, remaining thyme and sage and cook to reduce liquid by half. Add the cream and reduce until thickened (approximately 5 minutes). Return the veal to the pan and let simmer just until heated through (approximately 2 minutes). Transfer to serving platter and sprinkle with a little salt and pepper to taste and finish with fresh parsley. Serve.

Maple Pecan Chicken

Serves 4

MAPLE DIPPED CHICKEN WITH A TOASTED PECAN COATING. MY HUSBAND REQUESTED chicken for dinner one evening and I thought about doing something different. This is what I came up with and he really liked it. Now he requests it all the time.

- **4 boneless, skinless chicken breasts**
- **½ cup pecans, finely chopped**
- **¼ cup plain bread crumbs**

- **1 teaspoon black pepper**
- **½ teaspoon salt**
- **½ cup maple syrup**

1. Preheat oven to 350°F.

2. In a small bowl, mix together the pecans and bread crumbs. Transfer mixture to a shallow dish or plate. On a separate shallow dish or plate, pour the maple syrup.

3. Sprinkle each chicken breast with salt and pepper. Dip the chicken into the syrup, coating both sides completely, and then dip the chicken into the pecan and bread crumb mixture, coating both sides completely. Lay the chicken on a nonstick baking sheet and bake for 30-35 minutes.

Beef Tenderloins with Mushroom Sherry Sauce Serves 4

- **4 beef tenderloin steaks (approximately 4 ounces & 1 inch thick)**
- **½ cup shallots, finely chopped**
- **2 tablespoons butter**
- **½ cup sliced mushrooms**
- **½ cup steak sauce**
- **¼ cup sherry**
- **2 tablespoons chopped fresh Italian parsley**

1. In a medium saucepan over medium heat, sauté the shallots in the butter until tender. Stir in mushrooms and sauté for 1 minute. Stir in steak sauce and wine and heat to boil. Reduce the heat and let simmer for 10 minutes. Stir in the parsley. Set aside and keep warm.

2. In a separate pan over medium heat, grill the steaks for 3-4 minutes per side for medium-rare doneness. Plate the grilled steaks and drizzle the warm sauce over them.

Roasted Duck with Apple-Date Stuffing Serves 4

ROASTED DUCK STUFFED WITH APPLES, SWEET FIGS AND RUBBED WITH GARLIC. DUCK IS NOT often thought of when it comes to holidays or special occasions. Roasting turkeys and chickens have always taken the spotlight and the poor duck has been largely excluded. Duck meat is very distinguished and rich with flavor and I find the meat almost sweet. This recipe is one of my favorites.

- 1 whole duck (4 pounds)
- 1 garlic clove, halved
- 1 tablespoon unsalted butter
- 1 tablespoon olive oil
- 1 teaspoon fresh rosemary leaves, chopped
- 1 teaspoon fresh thyme leaves, chopped
- 1 teaspoon fresh sage leaves, chopped

- 1 cup fresh dates, pitted and chopped
- 4 sweet apples such as red delicious, pink lady, Gala
- ½ cup bread crumbs
- 1 egg beaten
- 1 tablespoon sugar
- 2-3 tablespoons dry red wine

1. Preheat oven to 400°F.

2. Rinse the duck thoroughly inside and out, with cool water and pat dry with paper towels. Rub the garlic, then the olive oil and butter over the skin of the duck. Sprinkle with the salt, pepper, rosemary, thyme and sage. Shred the apples using the large holes on a cheese grater, discarding the apple core and seeds. Place shredded apples in a large mixing bowl. Mix the dates, bread crumbs, egg, sugar, salt and a few tablespoons of wine to the apple mixture. Stuff the mixture into the cavity of the duck. Using twine, tie the legs of the duck together to close the stuffed cavity.

3. Bake for 2 to 2½ hours, covering the duck with foil for the first 1½ hours. Remove the foil and roast duck uncovered for remaining cook time. Baste occasionally with its own juices. Roast until duck meat reaches an internal temperature of 170°F to 180°F for well done. Remove and let sit for at least 10 minutes before cutting.

Herb-Roasted Leg of Lamb

Serves 8-10

LEG OF LAMB RUBBED WITH HERBS AND GARLIC AND ROASTED TO PERFECTION. I ALSO ADD potatoes and carrots to the pot to cook alongside the lamb. Not only does this create a one-pot meal, but the potatoes and carrots are flavored with the succulent juices from the lamb while they cook.

- 6 garlic cloves, minced
- 1 tablespoon fresh rosemary, chopped
- 1 tablespoon fresh thyme leaves
- 2 tablespoons butter, melted
- 1 (6 pound) leg of lamb (shank left in)

- 20-25 new potatoes, unpeeled
- 4 large carrots, cut into 1-inch pieces
- 2 tablespoons olive oil
- 2 teaspoons salt and pepper

1. In a small bowl, blend together the garlic, rosemary, butter, salt and pepper. Thoroughly coat the top and sides of the lamb with the mixture. Cover and let lamb sit at room temperature for at least 45 minutes to absorb flavors.

2. Preheat the oven to 450°F and move the oven rack to the center of the oven.

3. In a large roasting pan, toss the potatoes and carrots with the olive oil. Sprinkle with salt and pepper to flavor. Place the lamb on top of the potatoes and roast, uncovered, for 1 hour 15 minutes to 1 hour 30 minutes or until internal temperature of the lamb reaches 145° for medium doneness. Remove from oven and cover with foil. Allow lamb to rest for 20 minutes before slicing. Serve with potatoes and carrots.

Risotto with Wild Mushrooms, Peas and Mascarpone Cheese

Serves 6-8

PREPARING RISOTTOS CAN BE A LITTLE TIME CONSUMING, BUT THE CREAMY RICE REWARD IS worth it. This risotto is made with wild mushrooms, fresh peas and creamy mascarpone cheese.

- 5 ounces dried wild mushrooms (porcini, portabella, cremini, shiitake)
- 2 cups boiling water
- 7 cups chicken broth
- 2 tablespoons butter
- 2 tablespoon olive oil
- 1 cup chopped onion
- 4 garlic cloves, minced

- 2 cups Arborio rice or other medium-grain rice
- 1 cup dry white wine
- 1 teaspoon dried thyme
- ½ cup fresh green peas
- 1 cup grated Parmesan cheese
- ¼ cup mascarpone cheese
- ½ teaspoon salt
- ½ teaspoon black pepper

1. In a medium heat-safe bowl, combine the mushrooms and boiling water. Cover and let stand for 30 minutes or until mushrooms become tender. Drain, rinse and chop mushrooms. Set aside. In a large saucepan, add the broth and simmer.

2. Meanwhile, in a separate large saucepan over medium heat, warm the butter and oil. Add the onion and garlic to pan and cook for 8 minutes or until tender, stirring frequently. Add in the rice, salt and pepper and cook for 1 minute, stirring constantly. Add the wine and cook for 2 minutes or until liquid has absorbed, stirring constantly. Stir in mushrooms and thyme. Add the broth ½ cup at a time, stirring constantly until each portion of the broth is absorbed before adding the next amount. Continue to cook, adding more broth ½ cup at a time, stirring often (approximately 25-28 minutes total). Stir in peas, Parmesan cheese and mascarpone cheese. Season with a salt and pepper to taste. Enjoy.

Juicy Pork Tenderloin

Serves 6

PORK TENDERLOIN MARINATED IN VERMOUTH, GARLIC AND ROSEMARY, THEN roasted to perfection. No one will be able to resist this savory and juicy pork tenderloin.

- **2 pounds pork tenderloin**
- **½ cup vermouth**
- **2 garlic cloves minced**
- **2 tablespoons sugar**
- **3 tablespoons soy sauce**
- **1 teaspoonWorcestershire sauce**

- **½ teaspoon salt**
- **1 teaspoon black pepper**
- **3 tablespoons ketchup**
- **2 teaspoons fresh rosemary finely chopped**
- **cornstarch**

1. In a large dish or large plastic food bag, mix together the vermouth, garlic, sugar, soy sauce, Worcestershire sauce, salt, black pepper, ketchup and rosemary. Pour the mixture and rub into the meat. Refrigerate for 2 to 4 hours to marinate.

2. Preheat oven to 350°F.

3. Place pork on a rack in a large baking or roasting pan. Roast in oven for 35–45 minutes or until juices run clear when tested. Let stand for 10 minutes. Cut into thin slices and arrange on a serving platter. Transfer the roasting pan to the stovetop. Over low heat, add a little cornstarch, 1 tablespoon at a time. Cook for 1 minute, stirring frequently, to make the sauce. Pour over pork and serve.

Mediterranean Meatloaf

THIS RECIPE PROMISES TO BE THE JUICIEST AND MOST TENDER MEATLOAF. THE KEY IS TO ONLY use a small amount of bread crumbs. I find using too much absorbs the juices and flavors from the meat. I also add in my secret ingredient "Italian dressing" which makes it very moist. You can substitute the beef for ground chicken or turkey if you like—but I like the beef.

- 1 pound lean ground beef
- 1 large egg
- 1 small onion finely diced
- ¼ cup Italian dressing
- ¼ teaspoon salt
- 1 teaspoon black pepper
- 1 teaspoon parsley

- ½ teaspoon basil
- ½ teaspoon oregano
- ½ teaspoon thyme
- ¼ cup Italian Style bread crumbs
- ¼ cup feta cheese
- ½ cup marinara sauce

1. Preheat the oven to 375°F.

2. In a large bowl, add the beef, egg, onion, dressing, salt, pepper, basil, oregano, parsley, thyme, bread crumbs and ¼ cup of the feta cheese. Mix together until well blended. On a large baking sheet lined with foil, shape meat mixture into a loaf.

3. Transfer to the oven and bake for 55-60 minutes. Remove from oven and spread the marinara sauce over the top of the meatloaf and sprinkle with the remaining feta cheese. Return to oven and continue to cook for 5 minutes. Serve and enjoy the love.

Pork Chops In a Creamy Mushroom Sauce

Serves 4

PORK CHOPS COOKED IN A CREAMY MUSHROOM SAUCE. IT'S JUST THAT SIMPLE.

- **4 pork chops**
- **1 large onion, chopped**
- **1 tablespoon olive oil**
- **½ pound fresh mushrooms, sliced**

- **1 can (10 oz.) condensed cream of mushroom soup**
- **Salt and pepper**

1. Season the pork chops with salt and pepper. In a large saucepan over medium-high heat, add the oil, chops, onions and mushrooms. Cook for 1-2 minutes or until the onions and mushrooms are tender and the pork has browned on one side.

2. Turn the pork chops over and pour the cream of mushroom soup over the chops. Cover and reduce the temperature to medium-low. Simmer for 20-30 minutes or until chops are cooked through. Enjoy

Grilled Rib Eye Steak with Roquefort Sauce Serves 4

RIB EYE STEAKS CAN BE A LITTLE EXPENSIVE BUT THE TASTE IS WORTH IT. THEY'RE ONE OF the juiciest and most tender steaks to eat because of the cut and marbling. Rib eyes are very flavorful on their own but with this Roquefort sauce they're even better.

- **½ pound Roquefort cheese, softened**
- **½ cup unsalted butter, at room temperature**
- **1½ cup dry white wine**
- **4 teaspoons freeze-dried green peppercorns**

- **1 cup heavy cream**
- **4 teaspoons minced fresh Italian parsley**
- **1 pound (1-inch thick) rib eye steak**
- **salt and pepper**

1. In a medium bowl, mix the cheese and butter until smooth and creamy. Set aside.

2. In a medium saucepan, boil the wine with the peppercorns until it is reduced to about 1 tablespoon. Add the cream and boil the liquid until it has reduced by half. Lower the heat to medium-low and whisk in the cheese mixture gradually. Whisk in the parsley. Remove from heat and cover to keep warm.

3. Preheat a grill pan. Season the steak with salt and pepper. Grill steak for 4–5 minutes on each side for medium-rare. Remove from heat and let stand for at least 10 minutes before cutting. Slice into thin strips, across the grain, and arrange on a platter. Serve with Roquefort sauce.

Glazed Cornish Hens

I LOVE COOKING WITH CORNISH HENS. THEY'RE SO CUTE AND MAKE THE PERFECT PORTION size for everyone. Although I don't use a stuffing for this recipe, the hens can be stuffed with your favorite rice or bread mixture prior to cooking. When I do fill the cavity, I like to use wild rice and raisins.

- ½ cup mango chutney
- 1 tablespoon olive oil
- 4 teaspoons unsalted butter, divided
- 1 garlic clove, minced
- 1 teaspoon salt and pepper

- grated zest and juice of one large orange
- grated zest and juice of one large lemon
- 4 cornish hens (approximately 1½ pounds each)

1. Preheat oven to 350°F.

2. To make the glaze—in a small saucepan, combine the chutney, oil, 2 teaspoons butter, garlic, zest and juice of both the orange and lemon. Simmer for 5 minutes, breaking up any large mango pieces with a fork. Cut the orange and lemon into wedges and place a few into each of the hen's cavity.

3. Using twine, tie the legs of the hens together and turn the wing tips under. Arrange the hens, breast side up, in a baking dish. Rub the skin of each hen with the remaining butter and sprinkle with salt and pepper. Brush hens using a little of the mango glaze and reserve rest for basting.

4. Bake for 60-65 minutes or until hens are tender, basting hens occasionally with remaining glaze. Serve with rice and vegetables.

Pastas

Basic Marinara Sauce

THIS MARINARA RECIPE HAS BEEN USED OVER AND OVER SO MANY TIMES THAT I COULD make it in my sleep. Now, I know that it's easy to purchase marinara sauces from your local grocery store—and some are really good—but I like the taste of a homemade batch more and I also get great satisfaction making my own. There is one corner I cut to make the preparation a little easier, and that's by using canned chopped tomatoes—which are just as good as using fresh ones—and you don't have to spend the extra time boiling and blanching. I like to add mushrooms to my marinara sauce and sometimes olives. This version has mushrooms, but if you're not a big fan, feel free to exclude them… but they do add flavor. When preparing this sauce, I recommend making at least 2 batches, this way you can have some to freeze for whenever you may need it.

- ½ cup olive oil
- 1 medium onion, finely chopped
- 2 garlic cloves, finely chopped
- 2 celery stalks, finely chopped
- ½ cup cremini mushroom, finely chopped

- ½ teaspoon sea salt
- ½ teaspoon black pepper
- 2 (28 oz.) cans crushed tomatoes
- 2 dried bay leaves

1. In a large pot over medium-high heat, heat the oil. Add the onions and garlic and sauté until the onions are translucent (approximately 10 minutes). Add in the celery, mushrooms, salt and pepper and sauté until vegetables are soft (approximately 10 minutes). Add the tomatoes and bay leaves, and simmer uncovered over low heat, until the sauce thickens (approximately 1 hour). Remove and discard the bay leaves. Season the sauce with more salt and pepper. Remove from heat and let cool completely before transferring to jars.

2. Note—this sauce freezes well. I like to portion the sauce into small jars or plastic freezer bags and then freeze it. That way I don't have to thaw a huge jar if I only need a small amount.

Making Fresh Pasta

Makes approximately 1½ pounds

THERE ARE WONDERFUL FRESH PASTAS ALWAYS AVAILABLE AT THE LOCAL GROCERS, BUT I really enjoy making my own. It can take a little time and effort—and does require a pasta machine—but it's worth it. Pasta also freezes wonderfully, so make extra and stock up your freezer. When I make pasta, I like to add parsley or basil flakes to the dry flour mix before adding the eggs. This gives the pasta an herb-flavored taste and it also looks pretty… try it.

- · **3 cups all–purpose flour**
- · **4 large eggs, lightly beaten**
- · **1 teaspoon salt**
- · **1 tablespoon olive oil**

1. In a small bowl, combine the eggs, salt and oil together. Using a food processor, add the flour to the bowl and the egg mixture. Pulse to combine the ingredients, scraping down the sides (with the machine running), until the liquid is evenly distributed (approximately 1 minute). Check the dough by pinching it between your fingers to see if it sticks. Turn dough out onto a lightly floured surface, gather into a ball and gently knead until dough is smooth. Cover with plastic wrap and let rest for at least 30 minutes before rolling out.

Lasagna

LASAGNA...ONE OF THE MOST FAVORED AND FREQUENTLY SERVED ITALIAN DISHES. IT'S creamy, meaty, saucy and oh so good. I make it using marinara sauce—because that's the way it's mostly requested in my home—but it is traditionally made with both marinara and béchamel sauce. Either way, it's going to be a definite pleaser.

- 5 tablespoon olive oil
- 15 lasagna noodles
- 1 pound medium ground beef
- 1½ teaspoons salt
- 2½ teaspoon pepper
- 1 tablespoon Italian seasoning
- 2 teaspoons garlic powder
- 2 teaspoons onion powder
- 1 container of whole milk ricotta cheese (approx. 16 oz.)

- 3 large eggs
- 1 tablespoon unsalted butter
- 4 cups marinara sauce (homemade or your favorite jarred)
- 2 (10 oz.) packages frozen spinach, thawed and drained
- 1 cup shredded mozzarella cheese
- 1 cup shredded asiago cheese
- 1 cup grated Parmesan cheese

1. Bring a large pot of salted water to a boil. Add 2 tablespoons of olive oil to the water (a little oil in the water will prevent the noodles from sticking together). Add the lasagna noodles to the boiling water and cook until almost al dente (approximately 6 minutes). Drain and rinse noodles in cool water to stop cooking process and keep moist by wrapping them in a damp towel. Set aside.

2. In a large saucepan over medium-high heat, add 3 tablespoons of olive oil. Add the ground beef and cook meat until brown, breaking up any large clumps. Stir in 1 teaspoon of salt, 2 teaspoons of black pepper, Italian seasoning, garlic powder and onion powder. Remove from heat and drain any excess fat from the pan. Set aside. In a separate medium bowl, mix the ricotta, eggs and ½ teaspoon of salt and pepper together until blended. Set aside.

3. Preheat the oven to 375°F.

4. Coat the bottom of a large deep 13x9x5-inch baking dish with the butter. Spread approximately ¼ cup of the marinara sauce over the bottom of the dish. Place 5 of the cooked lasagna noodles (overlapping slightly) over the marinara sauce. Spread the ricotta cheese-egg mixture atop the noodles and top with spinach. Arrange 5 more noodles and spread the beef mixture on top of the noodles.

5. Spoon ½ of the marinara sauce atop the beef and spread ½ of all the shredded cheeses over top the marinara sauce. Arrange the last 5 noodles and spread the remaining marinara sauce on the noodles. Spread the remaining shredded cheeses and the Parmesan over the noodles and to finish the top.

6. Place lasagna on a heavy baking sheet lined with foil. Bake for 45 minutes or until lasagna is heated through and the cheese is bubbling. Remove and let stand for 10–15 minutes before slicing.

Basil Pesto

BASIL PESTO CAN BE USED IN MANY PASTA DISHES, APPETIZERS AND IT IS EVEN GREAT TO USE in marinades. There are so many uses for pesto and so many different flavors. I will usually take a day and spend it making all my marinaras, pastas and pestos. I make large amounts and freeze portions. I am also happy that I can now make this using my food processor. For years I used a mortar until I finally got a food processor, which saves so much time—not to mention my arms—now I can whip this up in no time.

- 2 cups fresh basil leaves
- ¼ cup toasted pine nuts
- 3 garlic cloves
- ½ teaspoon salt and pepper

- 5 ounces (2/3 cup) olive oil
- ½ cup freshly grated Parmesan cheese

1. To toast the pine nuts—Preheat the oven to 400°F. Spread the pine nuts out onto a baking sheet and bake for 5–10 minutes (but keep an eye them, because they can burn very quickly). Remove from oven and let cool.

2. Using a food processor, pulse the basil, pine nuts, garlic, salt and pepper until finely chopped. With the blender running, gradually add enough of the olive oil until mixture has formed into a smooth and thick consistency. Transfer the pesto to a medium bowl and stir in the Parmesan cheese. Season with more salt and pepper. Cover or pour into small jars and keep refrigerated.

Gnocchi with Sage Butter

Serves 6

ITALIAN DUMPLINGS WITH FRESH PARSLEY, CHIVES, SAGE AND PARMESAN CHEESE TOSSED IN A light butter sauce makes this dish simply delicious.

- **1 package (1 pound) fresh gnocchi**
- **3 tablespoons butter or margarine**
- **2 tablespoons fresh parsley, chopped**
- **2 tablespoons fresh chives, chopped**

- **1 teaspoon dried sage**
- **¼ teaspoon salt**
- **½ teaspoon black pepper**
- **¼ cup grated Parmesan cheese**

1. In a large pot of lightly salted boiling water, add the gnocchi. Cook for 2-3 minutes or until they begin to float to the surface. Drain and set aside. In a large saucepan, melt butter over low heat. Stir in parsley, chives, sage, salt and pepper and cook, stirring for 30 seconds.

2. Stir in gnocchi. Cook mixture until gnocchi is lightly browned and evenly coated with butter (approximately 4-5 minutes). Sprinkle with Parmesan cheese and cook, stirring until cheese has melted (about 1 minute). Remove from heat and serve.

Texan Stuffed Pasta Shells

TEXAS MEETS ITALY—AND WHAT A ZESTY BLEND! THE CREATIVITY AND IMAGINATION IS endless when stuffing pastas. I love trying new flavor combinations and this one has become a household favorite.

- 1 pound ground beef
- ⅔ cup fresh corn
- ⅔ cup ricotta cheese
- ½ cup mixed hot pepper rings
- 1 can (26 oz.) diced tomatoes with Italian spices
- 2½ cups prepared Thick and Chunky Salsa, medium boldness

- 1 package taco seasoning mix
- 1 cup water
- 2 cups packaged shredded Texan cheese mix
- 1 box (12 oz.) jumbo pasta shells
- 1 teaspoon butter
- salt

1. Bring a large pot of water to a rolling boil and add one tablespoon of salt. Add pasta shells and cook uncovered for 14–16 minutes. Shells should be firm prior to filling. Run under cold water and drain until cool enough to handle. Set aside.

2. Preheat oven to 350°F. Take a large, deep baking dish and coat the bottom evenly with butter, then spread a layer of 1½ cups of the diced tomatoes. Set aside.

3. In a saucepan, add the ground beef and cook thoroughly breaking up any large bits. Drain any excess fat and return to stove top. Add the taco seasoning and water to the beef and let simmer uncovered for 5 minutes until slightly thick, stirring often. Remove from heat, drain excess fluids and let cool. Add the corn, hot pepper rings, ricotta cheese and one cup of the salsa. Mix together until well blended.

4. Fill each pasta shell with beef blend and place in prepared baking dish aligning in rows until dish is full. Spoon 1½ cups of diced tomatoes and 1 cup salsa over the top of the shells and sprinkle with shredded cheese. Bake for 30 minutes. Serve with garlic bread.

Chicken Penne À La Carbonara

THIS PASTA IS SO GOOD AND SO FLAVORFUL. PENNE WITH CHICKEN, PANCETTA, PARSLEY and Parmesan cheese; the only important tip to remember when preparing this dish is to be sure to add the pancetta and cream mixture to the cooked pasta quickly, so the mixture will not curdle.

- 1 pound pancetta, diced into 1-inch cubes
- 3 boneless, skinless chicken breasts cut into ¼-inch strips
- 2 tablespoons olive oil
- 6 eggs
- ½ cup heavy cream (at room temperature)
- 1¼ cups freshly grated Parmesan cheese
- 1 pound penne noodles
- 2 tablespoons fresh parsley, chopped
- salt and pepper

1. Heat the oil in a large pan over medium-high heat. Add the pancetta and chicken and sauté until the pancetta is golden brown and crispy and the chicken is no longer pink (approximately 5 minutes). Season with salt and pepper and remove pan from heat.

2. In a bowl, beat together the eggs and cream. Add a little salt and pepper and stir in ¼ cup of the Parmesan cheese.

3. In a large pot of boiling salted water, add the pasta and cook until tender but still firm to the bite (approximately 8 minutes). Drain pasta, but do not rinse. While pasta is still hot, return it back to the pot and quickly add the browned pancetta and chicken, then the cream mixture and toss together (This is where it is important to work quickly so the cream mixture will cook but not curdle). Toss with the remaining cup of Parmesan cheese and the chopped parsley. Season with more salt and pepper and serve.

Lemon Fettuccini with Shrimp

Serves 4

THIS IS A NICE LIGHT PASTA DISH. I LIKE TO PREPARE AND SERVE THE SHRIMP LEAVING THE tails on, because I think it makes for a nicer presentation. Just be sure to remind your guests to remove them before eating.

- ⅔ cup olive oil
- ⅔ freshly grated Parmesan cheese
- ½ cup fresh lemon juice (2 lemons)
- 1 pound fettuccini noodles
- ⅓ cup chopped basil

- 1 tablespoon grated lemon zest from 2 lemons
- 1 pound large shrimp, cleaned, deveined (tails left on)
- 3 tablespoons olive oil
- salt and pepper

1. In a large bowl, add the oil, Parmesan cheese, lemon juice, ½ teaspoon of salt and 1 teaspoon of pepper. Whisk together and set aside.

2. In a large pot, bring salted water to a boil. Add the fettuccini, stirring occasionally until tender (approximately 8 minutes). Drain the pasta but do not rinse and reserve one cup of the cooking liquid. Add the fettuccini to the lemon sauce, add the basil and lemon zest and toss together.

3. In a pan over medium high heat, add 3 tablespoons of olive oil. Toss the shrimp with a little salt and pepper and sauté until the shrimp turn a light pink (approximately 2 minutes per side). Add the shrimp to the fettuccini and gradually add ¼ cup at a time, the reserved cooking liquid to the fettuccini and toss until moistened. Season with a little extra salt and pepper and transfer to a serving platter. Sprinkle with fresh basil and serve.

Penne with Prosciutto and Goat Cheese Serves 6

PROSCIUTTO IS AN ITALIAN HAM THAT HAS BEEN SEASONED, SALT-CURED, AND AIR-DRIED. It is often served raw "crudo" on antipasto plates and is usually wrapped around fresh fruits such as cantaloupes, honeydew, figs or even vegetables. It's also nice when served wrapped around breadsticks and fresh cuts of mozzarella cheese.

- 1 pound penne pasta
- 4 tablespoons olive oil
- 1 medium yellow onion, diced
- 3 garlic cloves, minced
- ¼ cup toasted almond slivers
- 4 ounces prosciutto, thinly sliced and cut into ½-inch pieces

- ¼ cup sliced sun dried tomatoes in oil, drained
- 1½ cups chicken broth
- ½ cup goat cheese, crumbled
- 8-10 fresh basil leaves
- salt and pepper

1. To toast the nuts—Preheat the oven to 400°F. Spread the nuts on a baking sheet and bake in the oven for 4-5 minutes or until lightly toasted (be sure to check on the nuts frequently because they can burn very quickly). Remove from oven and set aside.

2. In a large pot of lightly salted boiling water, add the pasta and cook until al dente (approximately 10 minutes). Drain but do not rinse, set aside.

3. In a large saucepan over medium heat, add the oil, garlic and onion. Sauté until the onion is tender but not browned (approximately 3 minutes). Add the prosciutto, basil and sun dried tomatoes. Toss together. Add the chicken broth and cook for 5-7 minutes. Add the pasta and goat cheese to the pan and stir together. Let mixture warm for 1 minute. Remove from heat and transfer to a serving dish. Season with salt and pepper and sprinkle with the toasted almonds. Serve hot.

Spaghetti and Meatballs

Serves 6

WHAT'S BETTER THAN A PLATE OF SPAGHETTI WITH BIG HOMEMADE MEATBALLS?

- ¼ cup bread crumbs
- 2 tablespoons chopped flat-leaf Italian parsley
- 2 eggs, lightly beaten
- 2 tablespoons milk
- ¾ cup grated Parmesan cheese

- ½ teaspoon salt and pepper
- 1 pound lean ground beef
- ¼ cup olive oil
- 5 cups marinara sauce
- 1 pound dried spaghetti

1. In a large bowl, add the bread crumbs, parsley, eggs, milk, ½ cup of Parmesan cheese, salt and pepper. Blend together. Add the ground beef and stir to combine. Shape the meat mixture to form medium-size meatballs.

2. Meanwhile bring a large pot of lightly salted water to a boil and add the spaghetti. Cook, stirring often, until tender but still firm to the bite (approximately 8 minutes). Drain but do not rinse pasta.

3. In a large saucepan, over medium-high heat, add the oil. Add the meatballs and cook without turning the meatballs until the bottoms have browned (approximately 3-4 minutes). Turn the meatballs over and brown the other side. Continue to cook until all sides are browned and the meatballs are cooked. Add the marinara sauce and bring to a boil. Reduce the heat and simmer, uncovered, for 5 minutes. Add the cooked pasta into the saucepan and mix to coat. Transfer to a large serving platter and sprinkle with remaining Parmesan cheese. Enjoy.

Pumpkin Ravioli with Walnuts

Serves 6

THE INGREDIENTS IN THIS RECIPE ARE DIFFERENT FROM THE TRADITIONAL FLAVORED RAVIOLI. The creamy, mildly sweet pumpkin filling matched with the warm butter and Parmesan cheese makes this truly unique. This is a great pasta to present around the holidays, but because the flavor is so good you'll want to enjoy this dish anytime.

- 1 can (18 oz.) pumpkin pie filling
- 1 can (3 oz.) evaporated milk
- 2 packages (18 oz.) wonton wrappesr
- ½ cup butter (1 stick)
- 1 cup chopped walnuts
- ⅔ cup grated Parmesan cheese
- 2 large eggs

1. For the filling, beat one egg lightly in a medium bowl. Add the pumpkin filling and evaporated milk. Blend together and pour batter into a 9x13-inch nonstick pan. Bake at 425°F for 15 minutes then reduce temperature to 375°F and continue baking 40-45 minutes or until knife inserted comes out clean. Cool completely.

2. To make the raviolis, drop teaspoon-sized amounts of filling onto the center of each wonton. Beat the second egg in a small bowl and brush egg wash on the edges of the wonton. Cover with a second wonton and gently press to remove air and to bind the edges.

3. Carefully keep the filling in the center and do not squeeze towards the edges or it will not form a good seal and will break apart when cooking. To ensure a secure bond and to make the edges look pretty, I like to cut around the wonton with a pastry cutter. Repeat this step for the rest of the wontons.

4. To cook, bring a large pot of water to a boil and add a teaspoon of salt. Drop the ravioli into the boiling water and let cook for approximately 3 minutes or until they float to the surface. Do not overcook. Then plate.

5. For the sauce, melt the butter over low heat. Stir in the Parmesan cheese to blend. Drizzle desired amount over the ravioli and top with chopped walnuts. Sprinkle with more Parmesan cheese if desired.

Baked Cheese Spinach Tortellini

Serves 6

BAKED PASTA DISHES ARE NOT ONLY TASTY BUT THEY'RE CONVENIENT. YOU CAN PICK UP THE prepared tortellini in your grocery store and have dinner on the table in less than an hour. Just put a few simple ingredients together, put it in the oven and it takes care of itself.

- 1 pound prepared cheese spinach tortellini
- 2 cups marinara sauce
- ½ cup ricotta or mascarpone cheese
- ¼ cup fresh parsley, chopped
- 1 tablespoon fresh thyme, chopped

- 2-3 ounces thinly sliced smoked mozzarella cheese
- ¼ cup grated Parmesan cheese
- 1 teaspoon olive oil
- salt and pepper to taste

1. Preheat oven to 350°F. Lightly oil a 9-inch baking dish.

2. In a large pot of lightly salted boiling water, cook the tortellini just until tender (approximately 2 minutes). Drain.

3. In a bowl, whisk together the marinara sauce, ricotta cheese, thyme, parsley, salt and pepper. Add the cooked tortellini to the sauce and toss together. Transfer the tortellini mixture to the baking dish and top with the mozzarella and Parmesan cheese. Cover the dish with foil and bake for 20 minutes. Remove foil and bake uncovered for 10 minutes or until the sauce bubbles and the cheese melts.

4. Serve with a tossed salad and enjoy.

Beef and Cheese Manicotti

I MAKE MANICOTTI FOR DINNER QUITE FREQUENTLY. IT'S HEALTHY, GOOD AND VERY satisfying. This recipe is for the more traditional version of manicotti, but I like to prepare it each time a little different. I will sometimes use ground chicken, spinach, mushrooms and different cheeses. It's hard to go wrong… so use your imagination and create different flavors.

- ½ pound lean ground beef
- 1 onion, finely chopped
- 1 container (approximately 15 oz.) ricotta cheese
- 2 garlic cloves, minced
- 1 cup shredded mozzarella cheese
- 1 teaspoon parsley
- 1 cup cheddar cheese

- ½ cup grated Parmesan cheese
- ½ teaspoon salt and pepper
- 1 tablespoon Italian seasoning
- 2 teaspoons olive oil
- 1 box manicotti pasta
- 1 cup marinara sauce
- ¾ cup béchamel sauce
- 1 tablespoon butter

1. Preheat oven to 350°F.

2. In a large saucepan over medium heat, add the ground beef, garlic and onion. Sauté until the meat browns and the onion is tender (approximately 5 minutes). Remove from heat and set aside.

3. In a bowl, mix the ricotta, ½ cup of the mozzarella and cheddar cheese, ¼ cup of the Parmesan cheese, parsley, seasoning, salt and pepper. Stir the meat mixture into the cheese mixture and set aside. Bring a large pot of lightly salted water to a boil. Working in batches, add the manicotti to the pot and cook until softened, but still firm (approximately 6 minutes). Remove manicotti from pot and place on a lightly oiled baking sheet to prevent sticking. Let cool. Repeat this procedure for the remaining manicotti.

4. Brush a 13x9-inch baking dish with the olive oil. Spoon ½ cup of the marinara sauce over the bottom of dish. When each manicotti shell is cool enough to handle, stuff each shell with the meat mixture using a spoon. Arrange stuffed pasta in a single layer in the prepared baking dish. Spoon the remaining marinara and béchamel sauce over the manicotti. Sprinkle the remaining mozzarella, cheddar and Parmesan cheese over the manicotti. Drop cut butter pieces on the top of manicotti. Bake uncovered for 35 minutes or until the sauce bubbles and cheese melts.

Chicken Pasta with Basil Pesto

Serves 4

THIS IS QUICK TO PUT TOGETHER, ONLY REQUIRING A FEW INGREDIENTS THAT ARE USUALLY already in the pantry. Simple and tasty.

- 1 pound Farfalle or penne pasta
- 1 tablespoon olive oil
- 4 boneless, skinless chicken breasts, cut into 1-inch pieces
- 1 can (8 oz.) artichoke hearts, drained and halved

- ½ cup basil pesto
- ½ cup chopped tomatoes
- ¼ cup grated Parmesan cheese

1. In a large pot of lightly salted boiling water, add the pasta and cook until tender but still firm to the bite (approximately 12 minutes). Drain and set aside.

2. Heat the oil in a large saucepan over medium-high heat. Add the chicken and cook for 4-5 minutes or until the chicken is no longer pink. Stir in the artichoke hearts, pesto and cooked pasta. Cook for 1-2 minutes or until heated through, stirring constantly. Stir in Parmesan cheese. Plate and sprinkle with chopped tomatoes. Enjoy.

Chicken Alfredo

THIS IS A LUSCIOUS AND CREAMY ALFREDO SAUCE MADE WITH RICOTTA CHEESE, CREAM and Parmesan cheese. You'll definitely be going back for seconds.

- **1 pound fettuccini pasta**
- **1½ cups butter, divided**
- **1 pound boneless, skinless chicken breasts, cut into slices**
- **2 (16 oz.) containers ricotta cheese**

- **2½ cups heavy cream**
- **1 teaspoon salt**
- **1 cup grated Parmesan cheese**

1. Bring a large pot of lightly salted water to a boil. Add the fettuccini and cook until al dente (approximately 8-10 minutes). Drain.

2. In a large saucepan over medium heat, melt 2 tablespoons of butter. Add the chicken and sauté until no longer pink (approximately 4-5 minutes). Remove chicken from the pan and set aside.

3. Using the same saucepan over medium heat, add the ricotta cheese, cream, salt, Parmesan cheese and remaining butter. Cook, stirring frequently until well combined (approximately 10 minutes). Stir in the chicken and fettuccini and heat through.

Farfalle with Asparagus, Mushrooms and Toasted Walnuts

THE NAME FARFALLE IS DERIVED FROM THE ITALIAN WORD "BUTTERFLY", BUT IS MORE commonly known as "Bow-tie" pasta. But don't let the fancy name fool you; this is definitely a no-fuss dish to make. If fresh asparagus is not in season, feel free to substitute them for fresh or frozen peas. They will work wonderfully with the other ingredients and will still give it that splash of color.

- 1 pound farfalle
- 1 pound cremini mushrooms, trimmed and sliced
- 1 pound of asparagus, trimmed and cut into 1-inch pieces
- 1 cup cream cheese
- ¾ cups walnuts toasted and chopped
- ¼ cup Parmesan cheese
- 1 tablespoon butter
- salt and pepper

1. To toast the walnuts—Preheat oven to 350°F. Spread coarsely chopped walnuts on baking sheet and bake for 10 minutes. Cool and set aside.

2. Bring a large pot of lightly salted water to a boil. Add the farfalle and cook until al dente, stirring occasionally (approximately 12 minutes). Drain but do not rinse and reserve 1 cup of the cooking liquid.

3. In a large saucepan over medium heat, melt the butter. Add the mushrooms and sauté until tender and their juices have partially evaporated (approximately 5 minutes). Add in the asparagus and sauté until slightly tender (approximately 5 minutes). Stir in the cream cheese. Add the cooked farfalle and stir until the cheese coats the pasta, gradually adding the reserved cooking liquid ¼ cup at a time to moisten. Stir in the toasted walnuts and ½ teaspoon of salt and 1 teaspoon of pepper. Transfer pasta to serving dish and sprinkle with Parmesan cheese. Enjoy.

Soups, Stews & Seafood

Cannellini Bean Soup with Tomatoes and Ditalini Pasta

A SIMPLE AND QUICK SOUP FULL OF TOMATOES, CANNELLINI BEANS, DITALINI PASTA, ONIONS, garlic and fresh parsley. Warm your tummy with this fabulous soup.

- 3 tablespoons olive oil
- 1 small onion, chopped
- 2 garlic cloves, minced
- 1 can (28 oz.) chopped tomatoes
- 1½ cups marinara sauce
- 1 can (15 oz.) cannellini beans, drained and rinsed

- 2 cups ditalini pasta (or other small pasta)
- 2 tablespoons fresh Italian flat-leaf parsley, chopped
- salt and pepper to taste

1. In a large pot, warm the olive oil over medium–high heat. Add the onion and garlic and sauté until soft (approximately 2 minutes). Add the tomatoes with juices, marinara sauce, beans and pasta. Simmer for 10 minutes. Stir in the parsley and season with salt and pepper to taste. Ladle into bowls and serve.

Wild Rice Soup

- **1 cup water**
- **½ cup wild rice**
- **1 pound lean ground beef**
- **1¼ cups condensed cream of mushroom soup**
- **1 cup chicken broth**
- **2 cups milk**

- **1 cup shredded cheddar cheese**
- **⅓ cup sliced cremini mushrooms**
- **1 (4 oz.) package of dry ranch salad dressing mix**

1. Add one cup of water to a medium pot and bring to boil. Add in the rice and cook for 10-12 minutes or until tender. Drain and Set aside. In a medium saucepan, over medium heat brown the beef, breaking up any large chunks. Drain off excess fat and stir in the cooked rice, chicken broth, cream of mushroom soup, milk, cheese, mushrooms and dry salad dressing mix. Blend together. Reduce heat to low and simmer covered for 15 minutes, stirring occasionally. Transfer to serving bowls and season with salt and pepper. Enjoy.

Soups, Stews & Seafood **85**

Veal Stew with Red Wine

THERE'S NOTHING LIKE COMING HOME TO A BIG POT OF COMFORTING STEW. THIS AROMATIC dish is full of rustic vegetables and hearty chunks of veal bathed in a thick and savory red wine sauce.

- 2 dozen cipollini onions
- 5 pounds veal stew meat
- ⅓ cup all-purpose flour
- 4 tablespoons olive oil
- 6 garlic cloves, finely chopped
- 1 tablespoon thyme leaves
- 2½ cups red wine
- 1 (14 oz.) can of diced tomatoes in juice
- 5 cups beef broth

- 1½ tablespoons tomato paste
- 20-24 small red-skinned potatoes, halved
- 2 large carrots, peeled and cut into 1-inch pieces
- 1 cup cremini mushrooms, stemmed and halved
- ¼ cup fresh Italian parsley, chopped
- 1 teaspoon salt and pepper

1. In a pot of boiling water, boil the onions for 2 minutes. Drain and let cool. When onions are cool enough to handle, peel and cut off the root end of each onion. Set aside. To prepare the veal, place the flour, salt and pepper in a sealable bag and add the veal chunks. Toss the veal with the flour to coat.

2. In a large heavy pot or Dutch oven, heat the oil over medium high heat. Working in batches, add the flour covered veal to the pot and cook until browned (approximately 10 minutes per batch), adding a little more oil if needed. As the veal browns remove to a plate and set aside. To the pot, add the garlic and thyme and sauté for 20-30 seconds. Add the wine and simmer over medium-high heat until liquid has reduced by half, stirring the bottom of the pot to loosen the bits (approximately 5 minutes). Add the veal back into the pot. Stir in the tomatoes and their juice, beef broth and tomato paste. Bring to a boil then reduce heat.

Partially cover and let simmer over medium-low heat for 20 minutes. Add the onion, potatoes, carrots and mushrooms to the stew. Let simmer uncovered until the veal and vegetables are tender and the stew has thickened (approximately 45 minutes). Plate and sprinkle with fresh parsley, and season with salt and pepper to taste. Serve with thick, crusty bread.

Note: Not all grocery stores carry cipollini onions. If you have difficulty finding them, just substitute the cipollini onions in this recipe with white or yellow pearl onions and prepare them the same way.

Chicken Noodle Soup

Serves 8

DURING THE COLD WINTER MONTHS THERE'S NOTHING COZIER THAN SNUGGLING UP ON the couch with a fluffy blanket, a great movie and a bowl of chicken noodle soup. I always make extra and freeze batches of it to have for whenever I want it. For this recipe I cut corners and make it even easier by using the already prepared roasted chickens that you can find at your local grocery store. Using ingredients that are already prepared can really save time without cutting out any of the flavor.

- 1 small purchased whole roasted chicken
- olive oil
- 2 quarts (10 cups) chicken stock
- 3 cups (about 3 stalks) chopped celery

- 3 large carrots, chopped into ½-inch pieces
- 2 cups wide egg noodles
- ¼ cup chopped fresh parsley
- salt and pepper to taste

1. Remove the skin from the roasted chicken and discard. Using a fork, shred the meat from the chicken and place in a bowl. Set aside (discard bones).

2. In a large pot, bring the chicken stock to a simmer. Add the celery, carrots and noodles. Simmer uncovered for 10 minutes or until the noodles are cooked. Add the shredded meat and parsley and heat through. Add salt and pepper to taste and serve with thick sliced bread.

Mom's Best Chili

Serves 6-8

MY MOM ALWAYS MADE THE BEST CHILI. LOVE YOU MOM.

- 3 pounds lean ground beef
- 1 large green pepper, chopped
- 1 large onion, chopped
- 2 (26 oz.) cans diced tomatoes
- 2 tablespoons tomato paste
- 1 cup water
- 1 teaspoon sugar

- 2 teaspoons cumin
- 3 teaspoons oregano
- ½ cup chili powder
- 1 can red kidney beans, drained and rinsed
- 1 can white kidney beans, drained and rinsed

1. In a large pot or Dutch oven over medium heat, add the ground beef and brown. Add the green peppers and onions and cook until slightly tender. Drain the excess fat.

2. Add the canned tomatoes with their juices, tomato paste, water, sugar, cumin, oregano, chili powder and beans to the pot and stir together. Reduce heat to low and simmer covered for 1 hour, stirring occasionally. If chili becomes too thick, add a little more water. Serve with crusty Italian bread and enjoy.

Ratatouille Stew

Serves 4-6

- 1 red bell pepper, chopped
- 1 zucchini, sliced lengthwise and chopped
- ½ medium eggplant, peeled and cut into small cubes
- 2½ cups canned whole tomatoes with juices, chopped

- 1 cup water
- 3 garlic cloves, minced
- 1 tablespoon Italian seasoning
- ½ cup orzo rice pasta

1. In a large saucepan over medium-high heat, combine the peppers, zucchini, eggplant, canned tomatoes, water, garlic and seasoning. Bring to a boil, then reduce heat to medium-low. Cover and cook for 15 minutes.

2. Add orzo rice, cover and cook for an additional 10-15 minutes or until orzo and vegetables are tender, stirring frequently. Serve with crusty bread.

Crispy Parmesan Fish

Serves 8

8 SKINNED WHITE FISH FILLETS SUCH AS HADDOCK, ORANGE ROUGHY OR FLOUNDER

- 8 white fish fillets, skinned
- 1 cup all-purpose flour
- 2 teaspoons paprika
- 1½ cups grated Parmesan cheese
- 2 cups bread crumbs
- 2 eggs, lightly beaten
- 4 tablespoons olive oil
- ½ cup butter (1 stick)
- 1 tablespoon grated lemon zest
- 1 tablespoon lemon juice
- 1 tablespoon fresh thyme, chopped
- salt and pepper

1. In a shallow dish, combine the flour, paprika salt and pepper. In a separate shallow dish, combine the Parmesan and bread crumbs. Dredge fish with the flour, coating both sides. Dip coated fish into the beaten eggs and then the Parmesan and bread crumb mix. Transfer to a plate and set aside.

2. In a large frying pan over medium heat, add the oil. Working in batches, cook the fish (approximately 3-5 minutes per side). Transfer cooked fish to a plate and tent with foil to keep warm.

3. In the same frying pan, add the butter, lemon rind, lemon juice and thyme. Heat and stir until butter has melted. Drizzle a little of the butter sauce over the warm fish. Transfer the remaining sauce into a separate bowl and serve along with the fish.

Swordfish in Tomato Sauce with Garlic

Serves 6

SWORDFISH HAS A NICE DENSE TEXTURE THAT'S FILLING AND MEATY. THESE STEAKS ARE made with tomato sauce, mushrooms and capers and it's good.

- **6 swordfish steaks**
- **2 tablespoons olive oil**
- **2 tablespoons basil**
- **½ cup fresh Italian parsley, chopped**
- **2 garlic cloves, minced**

- **1 cup tomato sauce**
- **¾ cup sliced mushrooms**
- **1 tablespoon capers**
- **1 tablespoon lemon juice**
- **1 teaspoon black pepper**

1. Preheat oven to 400°F.

2. In a medium saucepan over medium heat, add the oil, basil, parsley and garlic. Sauté for 1 minute, then reduce heat to low. Add in the tomato sauce and mushrooms. Simmer uncovered for 5 minutes.

3. Stir in lemon juice and pepper. In a baking dish, place the swordfish side by side in a single layer and cover with sauce. Bake for 20 minutes or until fish flakes easily when tested with fork.

Cajun Baked Fish

Serves 4

CAJUN SEASONING ADDS A DELICIOUS SPICY FLAVOR TO THESE SALMON FILLETS. TRY IT FOR YOURSELF.

- 4 salmon fillets
- 2 tablespoons olive oil
- 2 teaspoons garlic salt
- 2 teaspoons thyme

- 2 teaspoons paprika
- ½ teaspoon cayenne pepper
- ½ teaspoon Tabasco sauce
- ½ teaspoon black pepper

1. Preheat oven to 425°F.

2. In a small bowl, combine the canola oil, garlic salt, thyme, paprika, cayenne, Tabasco sauce and black pepper. Place the salmon in a baking dish and brush each fillet with mixture.

3. Bake for 17-20 minutes or until fish flakes easily with a fork. Serve with steamed vegetables or rice.

Hazelnut Coated Salmon

Serves 4

SALMON IS MY FAVORITE FISH TO EAT. IT HAS SUCH A RICH FLAVOR THAT IS ALMOST SWEET. This hazelnut coated salmon is so scrumptious that it will make you a salmon lover too.

- ½ cup hazelnuts
- 4 salmon fillets
- 1 tablespoon apple butter
- 1 tablespoon grainy mustard

- ¼ teaspoon thyme
- ¼ teaspoon rosemary
- ½ teaspoon black pepper

1. To toast hazelnuts—Preheat oven to 375°F. Place hazelnuts on baking sheet and bake in oven for 8-9 minutes or until lightly browned. Remove from oven and quickly put in a dry, clean dish towel and rub vigorously to remove skins. Finely chop nuts using a food processor. Set aside.

2. Increase oven temperature to 450°F.

3. In a small bowl, combine the apple butter, mustard, thyme, rosemary and pepper. Arrange fillets, skin side down, into a baking dish. Brush butter-mustard mixture overtop each fillet and top with the ground hazelnuts. Bake for 14-16 minutes. Serve with steamed vegetables and brown rice.

Broiled Salmon with Honey Mustard Sauce Serves 4

WE EAT A LOT OF SALMON. IT'S TASTY AND GOOD FOR YOU. SALMON IS VERY VERSATILE and can be topped with a variety of flavors. Hot salsa sauce or mayonnaise with lemon and dill are some of our household favorites, but salmon with honey mustard sauce is the most requested.

- **4 salmon fillets**
- **1 teaspoon lemon juice**
- **1 teaspoon mayonnaise**
- **1 tablespoon grainy mustard**
- **½ teaspoon rosemary**

- **½ teaspoon thyme**
- **1 tablespoon honey**
- **1 teaspoon butter**
- **1½ teaspoons olive oil**
- **salt and pepper**

1. Preheat the broiler.

2. In a small bowl, combine mustard, lemon juice, mayonnaise, rosemary and thyme. Mix in the honey and butter. Set aside.

3. Place the salmon fillets on a heavy nonstick baking sheet. Lightly coat with olive oil and sprinkle with salt and pepper. Place under broiler and cook for 2 minutes. Remove from oven. Spoon the mustard sauce over the fillets and place back under broiler and cook until the fillets are cooked through, and a golden brown crust has formed on the top (approximately 4-5 minutes). Plate and serve with lemon wedges.

Macadamia Nut Covered Shrimp

Serves 4

JUMBO SHRIMP BAKED IN A TASTY CRISPY COATING OF MACADAMIA NUTS. YOU WILL LOVE them. Serve with warm mango or peach chutney for dipping.

- **1 pound jumbo shrimp, devein and cleaned (leave tails on)**
- **1 cup macadamia nuts**
- **⅓ cup plain dry bread crumbs**
- **½ teaspoon salt**
- **½ teaspoon cayenne pepper**
- **2 egg whites, lightly beaten**

1. Preheat oven to 450°F.

2. Using a food processor, add the nuts, bread crumbs, salt and cayenne pepper. Mix until the nuts are ground. Transfer mixture to a shallow dish.

3. Dip shrimp into egg whites, letting excess drip off, then dip egg covered shrimp into ground nut mixture to coat. Place shrimp on a baking sheet and lightly mist with cooking spray.

4. Bake for 5 minutes, then remove from oven and turn shrimp. Lightly mist shrimp again with cooking spray and bake for another 5 minutes or until coating has browned.

Drunken Mussels with White Wine and Tomatoes Serves 4

MUSSELS WITH GARLIC, WINE AND JUICY TOMATOES. THIS IS GREAT SERVED OVER SPAGHETTI or my favorite… just as they are, with lots of crusty bread for soaking up the sauce.

- 4 pounds live mussels
- 2 tablespoons unsalted butter
- 1 tablespoon olive oil
- 1 medium onion, chopped
- 4 garlic cloves, minced
- 1½ cups dry white wine
- 2 cans (16 oz.) chopped plum tomatoes, drained
- ½ cup fresh Italian parsley, chopped
- salt and pepper

1. Fill the sink ½ full of cold water. Add the mussels and toss them around. Let them soak for 30 minutes or until the mussels disgorge any sand. Pull the beards and scrape off any barnacles from each mussel (inspecting them to make sure that they are tightly closed). Discard any bad mussels. Transfer the cleaned mussels to a bowl and refrigerate until ready for use.

2. In a large pot, heat the butter and oil over medium heat. Add the onions and cook for 5 minutes. Add the garlic and cook until the onion is translucent (approximately 3 minutes). Add the wine, tomatoes, parsley, salt and pepper. Bring to a boil.

3. Add the mussels, stir well, then cover and cook over medium heat, until all the mussels are opened (approximately 8-10 minutes). Discard any that do not open. Pour the mussels and sauce into bowls and serve immediately.

Roasted Red Snapper with Tomatoes, Onions and Thyme

Serves 4

PRESENTING A WHOLE ROASTED FISH WILL DEFINITELY IMPRESS YOUR GUESTS. THIS delicious fish is quick and easy to prepare, and the flavors along with the amazing presentation will definitely leave an impact on your guests.

- 1 (6 pound) whole red snapper, scaled and cleaned
- 1 medium onion, chopped
- 6 garlic cloves, thinly sliced
- 2 plum tomatoes, seeded and sliced
- ½ fennel bulb, coarsely chopped

- ½ green bell pepper, sliced
- 1 lemon, cut into 4 wedges
- 4 sprigs fresh thyme
- 4 springs fresh flat-leaf parsley
- 4 tablespoons olive oil
- salt and black pepper

1. Preheat the oven to 400°F.

2. Lightly oil the bottom of a large roasting pan or deep baking sheet. Rinse the fish inside and out with cold water and pat dry. Sprinkle the cavity of the fish with salt and pepper. Squeeze the lemon wedges inside the fish cavity and then place them inside the fish. Fill the cavity with the tomatoes, onions, fennel, bell pepper, garlic, thyme and parsley (if there is additional mix that will not fit into the cavity, just spoon the remainder around the fish). Rub a little olive oil over the fish and sprinkle with salt and pepper.

3. Roast in the oven until the fish is cooked through (approximately 40 minutes). If you are using a smaller sized fish (around 2-3 pounds), cook for approximately 20-30 minutes.

4. To Serve—Pull back the skin from atop the fish. Use a long, sharp thin-blade knife and cut vertically through the top fillet to the backbone. Make an incision down the backbone and remove the dorsal fins. Use a large fork to lift off the 2 portions of the top fillets and plate. Lift off the bone structure and head and discard. Cut the bottom fillet in half horizontally and plate. Serve with cooked vegetables, rice and crusty bread.

Breads &
Cereals

Granola

I LOVE THIS WITH MILK OR SPRINKLED OVER YOGURT BUT IT'S EVEN GREAT ON ITS OWN eaten by the handful. The cinnamon gives it a sweet flavor and a homemade aroma.

- **4 cups old fashioned rolled oats**
- **2 cups shredded sweetened coconut**
- **2 cups sliced almonds**
- **1 cup brown sugar**
- **1 tablespoon ground cinnamon**

- **½ cup honey**
- **1½ cups dried pineapple, chopped**
- **1 cup dried cherries**
- **1 cup golden raisins**
- **1 cup dried dates**
- **¾ cup vegetable oil**

1. Preheat oven to 350°F.

2. In a large bowl, toss the oats, coconut, almonds, brown sugar and cinnamon together. In a separate bowl, whisk the oil and honey together. Pour the honey-oil mixture over the oat mixture and stir with wooden spoon until the dry mixture is coated with the honey-oil. Spread evenly on a large 13x18-inch baking sheet and bake until golden brown (approximately 35-40 minutes). Check the mixture every so often and make sure to stir occasionally to ensure even browning.

3. Remove granola from oven and allow to cool. When cooled, add the pineapple, cherries, raisins and dates. Mix together and store in an airtight container.

Marathon Bars

Makes 12 Bars

When preparing and training for marathons, I fuel myself with protein bars and energy drinks. This is my protein bar recipe that I like to use for the energy kick needed while training and competing.

- **1 cup of whey protein powder**
- **½ cup oat bran**
- **⅔ cup whole-wheat flour**
- **½ teaspoon salt**
- **½ cup dark raisins**
- **½ cup dried cherries**
- **½ cup dried apricots**
- **½ cup dried dates**

- **1 package soft tofu**
- **½ cup apple juice**
- **½ cup brown sugar**
- **2 large eggs, beaten**
- **⅔ cup smooth peanut butter**
- **½ cup slivered almonds**
- **1 tablespoon canola oil**

1. Line the bottom of a 13x9-inch glass baking dish with parchment paper and lightly coat with canola oil.

2. Preheat oven to 350°F. In a large bowl, combine the protein powder, oat bran, wheat flour and salt. Set aside.

3. Coarsely chop the dried fruit and nuts and place in a small bowl. In a separate bowl, whisk the tofu until smooth. Add the apple juice, brown sugar and peanut butter. Add in eggs one at a time and whisk to combine after each addition. Add this to the protein powder mixture and stir well to combine. Fold in the dried fruit and nuts and spread evenly in the prepared baking dish. Bake for 35 minutes. Remove from oven and cool completely. Cut into 4 inch bars and store in an airtight container for up to one week.

Banana Bread

OF ALL THE BREADS TO BAKE AND EAT, BANANA IS MY FAVORITE. MY MOM'S TIP FOR achieving the intense banana flavor is to use very ripe bananas.

- ½ cup (1 stick) unsalted butter, softened
- 2 cups all-purpose flour
- 1 teaspoon baking powder
- ½ teaspoon baking soda
- ½ teaspoon of salt
- ½ teaspoon cinnamon

- 1 teaspoon vanilla extract
- ¾ cup sugar
- 3 large ripe bananas, peeled and sliced
- 2 eggs
- ¼ cup milk
- ¼ cup chopped walnuts

1. Preheat oven to 350°F.

2. In a medium saucepan over low heat, melt the butter. Remove from heat, add the sliced bananas and mash with fork until mushy. In a large bowl, sift together the flour, baking powder, baking soda, salt, cinnamon and sugar.

3. In a separate medium bowl, whisk together the eggs, vanilla and milk. Add the banana mixture and the whisked eggs to the flour mixture. With a wooden spoon, blend all ingredients. Do not over mix batter. Add walnuts and stir just until blended.

4. Pour batter mix into a nonstick 9x5x3-inch loaf pan. Bake for 55–60 minutes or until a toothpick comes out clean when inserted in the center. During the baking process rotate the bread in the oven once halfway between the baking time to ensure the bread rises evenly. Cool completely on rack before removing from pan.

Onion - Zucchini Bread

I SERVE THIS ALONGSIDE MANY DINNER ENTREES. I APPRECIATE THE PREPARED LOAVES THAT ARE AVAILABLE AT THE GROCERY STORE, BUT NOTHING COMPARES TO HOME BAKED. ONIONS, ZUCCHINI, PARMESAN CHEESE, BASIL AND PARSLEY MAKE THIS BREAD A WINNER.

- 1 large zucchini (or 2 small), shredded
- 2½ cups all-purpose flour
- ½ cup dried onion flakes
- ½ cup grated Parmesan cheese
- 1 tablespoon baking powder
- 1 tablespoon basil

- 1 tablespoon parsley
- ½ teaspoon salt
- 1 cup milk
- ½ cup (1 stick) unsalted butter, melted
- 2 tablespoons light brown sugar
- 2 eggs

1. Preheat oven to 350°F.

2. To prepare the zucchini—Grate zucchini with a cheese grater, using the medium or small holes. Drain in a colander, then place in cheese cloth (or a kitchen towel) and squeeze out excess liquid. Set aside.

3. In a large bowl, mix the flour, onion flakes, cheese, baking powder, basil, parsley and salt. In a separate medium bowl, whisk together the milk, butter, brown sugar and eggs. Stir the zucchini into the milk mixture.

4. Add milk-zucchini mixture to the flour mixture, stirring just until moistened. Do not over mix. Pour batter into prepared nonstick 9x5x3-inch loaf pan. Run a knife down the center of batter.

5. Bake for 50 minutes or until golden and a toothpick comes out clean when inserted in the center. Let cool. Slice and serve. This is great with garlic butter.

Fruit and Nut Muffins

Makes 1 Dozen

APPLES, DATES, BANANAS, AND WALNUTS. THESE MUFFINS ARE TASTY, NOT TOO SWEET, AND FULL OF HEALTHY INGREDIENTS. START OFF YOUR MORNING WITH ONE TODAY.

- 1 cup whole-wheat flour
- 1 cup all-purpose flour
- ½ cup sugar
- 2 teaspoons baking powder
- 2 teaspoons cinnamon
- ½ teaspoon baking soda
- ½ teaspoon salt
- ½ cup buttermilk

- ½ cup vegetable oil
- 1 ripe banana, mashed
- 1 egg
- ½ cup chopped dates
- ½ cup chopped dried figs
- 1 apple, peeled, cored and chopped
- ½ cup chopped walnuts

1. Preheat oven to 375°F.

2. In a large bowl, combine the whole-wheat flour, all-purpose flour, sugar, baking powder, cinnamon, baking soda and salt. In a separate large bowl, mix the buttermilk, oil, mashed banana and egg. Add the buttermilk-banana mixture to the flour mixture and lightly blend together.

3. Add in the dates, figs, apple and nuts and mix just until blended. Spoon batter into prepared muffin cups, filling almost to the top, and bake for 25 minutes or until a wooden toothpick comes out clean when inserted in the center of muffin. Let cool before removing from tray.

Coconut Bread with Creamy Pineapple Butter Makes 1 Loaf

I BROUGHT THIS OVER TO MY FRIEND'S HOUSE AND THE GIRLS WENT CRAZY FOR IT.
So here's the recipe—serve with caution!

- Bread:
- 1½ cups shredded sweetened coconut, toasted
- 3 cups all-purpose flour
- 1 tablespoon baking powder
- ½ teaspoon baking soda
- ½ teaspoon salt
- 1 teaspoon ground cinnamon
- ½ cup (1 stick) unsalted butter, melted
- 1 cup brown sugar packed
- 2 eggs, lightly beaten

- 1 teaspoon vanilla extract
- 1 teaspoon lemon zest
- 1½ cups unsweetened coconut milk
- confectioners sugar for dusting

Pineapple Butter:
- 1 can crushed pineapple, drained
- 1 cup (2 sticks) unsalted butter, softened

1. To toast coconut—preheat oven to 350°F. Spread coconut evenly on cookie sheet. Bake for 10 minutes or until coconut is a light golden brown (toasted coconut will fluff and increase volume of bread). Set aside.

2. Preheat oven to 375°F. In a large bowl, sift together the flour, baking powder, baking soda, salt and cinnamon. In a separate large bowl, whisk together the melted butter with the brown sugar, eggs, vanilla and lemon zest. Pour in the coconut, milk and whisk together. Pour wet ingredients into the dry ingredients and fold everything together with a spatula until you have a smooth batter.

3. Gently fold in the shredded coconut until evenly distributed. Pour into a nonstick 9x5x3-inch loaf pan and bake for 1 hour or until wooden toothpick comes out clean when inserted into the center of the bread. Rotate the loaf once halfway between baking time to ensure even browning. Cool the bread in the pan before removing.

4. Butter Preparation: Press the liquid out of the crushed pineapple. In a bowl, mash the pineapple with the softened butter until well blended. Toast a slice of bread, dust with confectioners sugar and serve with pineapple butter.

Sweet Potato Biscuits

I LOVE TO BAKE BISCUITS; THEY'RE A GREAT ALTERNATIVE TO MINI BUNS OR ROLLS. THESE biscuits are made with mashed sweet potatoes, pecans, cinnamon and ginger. Serve these up with your next turkey dinner and watch them disappear.

- 2½ cups all-purpose flour
- ¼ cup brown sugar
- 1 tablespoon baking powder
- ½ teaspoon salt
- 1 teaspoon ground cinnamon
- ½ teaspoon ground ginger
- ½ teaspoon allspice

- ½ cup (1 stick) unsalted butter
- ½ cup chopped pecans
- ¾ cup mashed canned sweet potatoes
- ½ cup milk

1. Preheat oven to 450°F.

2. In a large bowl, combine the flour, sugar, baking powder, salt, cinnamon, ginger and allspice. Using a pastry blender or two knives, cut in the butter until mixture resembles coarse crumbs. Stir in pecans.

3. In a separate large bowl, whisk together the sweet potatoes and milk until smooth. Form a well in the center of the flour mixture and add sweet potato mixture. Stir until mixture forms soft dough that sticks together forming a ball.

4. Turn dough onto a well-floured surface and knead gently. Do not over handle. Roll or pat dough until it is ½-inch thick. Cut with a biscuit cutter or knife to make 2½-inch biscuits.

5. Place biscuits on nonstick baking sheet and bake for 12 minutes or until tops and bottoms are golden brown.

Chocolate Macadamia Muffins

Makes 1 Dozen

BECAUSE THESE MUFFINS ARE SO GOOD AND DISAPPEAR SO QUICKLY... I HAVE TO BAKE THEM often and in very large batches.

- 1½ cups milk
- ⅓ cup vegetable oil
- 1 cup sugar
- 1 egg, beaten
- 1 tablespoon molasses
- 1 teaspoon vanilla extract
- 3 cups all-purpose flour

- 3 tablespoons unsweetened cocoa powder
- 2 teaspoons baking powder
- 1½ teaspoons baking soda
- 1 teaspoon salt
- 1 cup chocolate chips
- 1 cup macadamia nuts, chopped

1. Preheat oven to 375°F.

2. In a medium bowl, combine the milk, oil, sugar, egg, molasses and vanilla. Stir until sugar is dissolved. Set aside.

3. In a separate large bowl, mix the flour, cocoa powder, baking soda, baking powder and salt. Pour the milk mixture into the flour mixture and stir together. Add in the chocolate chips and nuts and blend until combined. Pour into prepared muffin cups and bake for 25-28 minutes or until toothpick comes out clean.

Strawberry Banana Pancakes

PANCAKES ARE ONE OF MY FAVORITE BREAKFAST TREATS. IN OUR HOME, EVERY SUNDAY morning we have pancakes. We pick which fruit or flavor combinations we want and make stacks of them. We'll choose anything from cut up fruit, chocolate chips and even candies, try it… you'll want to make this a weekend treat too.

- 1½ cups all-purpose flour
- 3½ teaspoon baking powder
- ½ teaspoon salt
- 1 tablespoon sugar
- 1 egg, lightly beaten
- 1¼ cups milk

- 3 tablespoons unsalted butter, melted
- ½ cup strawberries, thinly sliced
- ½ banana, thinly sliced

1. In a large bowl, sift together the flour, baking powder, salt and sugar. Form a well in the center and pour in the milk, egg and melted butter and mix together until smooth. Mix in the strawberries.

2. Heat a lightly-oiled griddle or frying pan over medium heat. Pour or scoop batter onto pan (approximately ¼ cup in size). Fry until brown turning only once. Top with maple syrup and banana slices.

To make chocolate pancakes, just add 1 tablespoon of cocoa powder to the batter.

Three Grain Cereal Bars

Makes 30 Bars

HERE'S AN EASY AND QUICK RECIPE TO MAKE YOUR OWN BREAKFAST BARS, WHICH ARE great for when you're always on the go.

- **4 cups bran flake cereal**
- **3 cups wheat square cereal**
- **2 cups toasted O's cereal**
- **¾ cup smooth peanut butter**

- **½ cup corn syrup**
- **2 tablespoons unsalted butter**
- **25 large marshmallows**

1. In a large bowl, combine the cereals and set aside. In a medium saucepan, combine the peanut butter, corn syrup, margarine and marshmallows. Cook over low heat until marshmallows are melted, stirring constantly.

2. Pour marshmallow mixture over the cereal mixture and mix until well blended. Using a butter coated spatula, press mixture into a nonstick 13x9-inch pan. Cool and cut into bars. Store in an airtight container and refrigerate.

Cranberry Orange Walnut Bread

Makes 1 Loaf

BREADS ARE GREAT TO MAKE BECAUSE YOU CAN ADD ALMOST ANY DRIED FRUITS AND NUTS desired. This one is made with dried cranberries and walnuts, but try using dried dates, pineapple or raisins.

- 2 cups all-purpose flour
- 1 cup rolled oats
- ¼ cup sugar
- 1 teaspoon baking powder
- ½ teaspoon baking soda
- ¼ cup grated walnuts
- ½ teaspoon salt
- ¾ cup milk

- 3 large eggs
- ⅓ cup orange juice, unsweetened
- 1 tablespoon grated orange peel
- ¼ cup vegetable oil
- ¾ cup dried cranberries
- ¼ cup chopped walnuts

1. Preheat oven to 350°F.

2. In a large bowl, sift together the flour, oats, sugar, baking powder, baking soda, grated walnuts and salt. In a separate medium bowl, beat the milk, eggs, orange juice, orange peel and vegetable oil until thoroughly mixed.

3. Add the dry ingredients to the wet mixture, mixing until moistened. Do no over mix. Stir in the cranberries and walnuts. Pour batter into a nonstick 9x5x3-inch loaf pan and bake for 60-70 minutes or until a wooden toothpick inserted in the center comes out clean. Cool loaf completely on rack before removing from pan.

Sweet Treats

Chocolate Truffles

THESE LITTLE CHOCOLATE DELIGHTS ARE A NICE AFTER DINNER TREAT, BUT ALSO MAKES for a great gift idea. I like placing the truffles in pretty candy cups and packaging them in elegant boxes or glass jars with a big bow. Get creative and roll truffles in different coatings like nuts, icing sugar or even coconut. Then wrap them up and give them to the next party host or hostess.

- **½ cup whipping cream 35%**
- **7 ounces dark semisweet chocolate, chopped finely**

- **ground almonds, cocoa powder and icing sugar for coating truffles**

1. In a heavy pot over medium heat, add the whipping cream and bring to a boil, stirring constantly, until cream has reduced by half (approximately 10 minutes). The cream may start to boil over, just reduce heat but keep cream boiling.

2. Remove from heat and add chopped chocolate, stirring until smooth. Transfer mixture to a shallow container and refrigerate until firm (approximately 4-5 hours), do not cover. To shape truffles—Using a small melon baller or spoon, scoop out 2 teaspoons of the cold mixture and form into a ball by rolling it between your palms. Roll each ball in the topping of your choice and place on a platter. Cover and keep refrigerated until ready to serve.

Flourless Chocolate Torte

Serves 12

PURE DECADENCE; YOU'LL ONLY NEED A SLIVER OF THIS TORTE TO EXCITE YOUR TASTE buds. I know this recipe may seem like a lot of work... but trust me, it will be worth it.

- **Torte:**
- **1 pound unsalted butter**
- **1 pound semisweet chocolate squares, chopped**
- **1 cup whipping cream**
- **1 cup sugar**
- **9 large eggs**

- **4 teaspoons vanilla**
- **Topping:**
- **1 cup whipping cream**
- **12 ounces semisweet chocolate squares, chopped**
- **cocoa powder for dusting**

1. Preheat oven to 350°F.

2. In a large saucepan, combine the 1 pound chocolate, butter, 1 cup whipping cream and sugar. Cook and stir over medium heat until chocolate and butter melt. Remove and set aside.

3. In a large bowl, whisk the eggs and the vanilla together. Slowly stir in half of the chocolate mixture into the egg mixture. Return egg mixture to remaining chocolate mixture and stir until combined. Pour batter into nonstick 10-inch springform pan and bake in oven for 45–50 minutes or until evenly puffed and knife inserted in center comes out clean. Remove from oven and cool completely on rack. Chill in fridge for several hours until firm. Remove chilled torte from springform pan and plate.

4. To make Topping—In a saucepan, heat 1 cup whipping cream just until it begins to boil then remove from stovetop. Place the 12 ounces of chocolate in a medium bowl. Add the hot whipping cream to the chocolate and stir until melted. Cool mixture to room temperature. Spread the chocolate over the top of the torte allowing some of the mixture to drizzle down the sides. Cover and chill for at least 20 minutes or until set. Dust top with cocoa powder, covering completely.

Kahlúa Fudge Brownies

Makes 1 Dozen

I LOVE CHOCOLATE AND ANYTHING MADE WITH IT. THESE BROWNIES WILL SURELY SATISFY any chocoholic's craving. Rich, thick and nutty brownies with a touch of Kahlua to give it that ultimate wow.

- 4 ounces unsweetened chocolate
- 1 cup (2 sticks) unsalted butter
- 4 large eggs, lightly beaten
- 1½ cups sugar
- 1½ teaspoons vanilla extract

- 1/3 cup Kahlúa
- 1 tablespoon coffee grounds
- 1⅓ cups all-purpose flour
- dash of salt
- ¼ teaspoon baking powder
- 1 cup chopped walnuts (optional)

1. Preheat oven to 350°F.

2. Melt the chocolate squares and butter over low heat, stirring until smooth. Remove from heat and allow the mixture to cool slightly.

3. Combine the eggs, sugar and vanilla in a large bowl. Beat well. Stir in the cooled chocolate mixture, Kahlúa and coffee. Combine the flour, salt and baking powder and add to the chocolate mixture. Mix together until well blended. Add the walnuts and spread batter evenly into a nonstick 9-inch baking pan.

4. Bake in oven for 25 minutes (do not over bake). Remove from oven and let cool completely before cutting into squares.

Chocolate Marshmallow Coconut Balls

THESE LIGHT, CHOCOLATE AND MARSHMALLOW TREATS WHERE MY GRANDFATHERS favorite. We would make batches of these and take them over to Grandpa's house as a surprise.

- · 1 (8 oz.) package cream cheese (room temperature)
- · 2 tablespoons milk
- · 2 cups icing sugar
- · 2 (1 oz.) semisweet chocolate squares, melted

- · 1 teaspoon vanilla
- · 3 cups mini marshmallows
- · 4 cups shredded unsweetened coconut
- · dash of salt

1. In a small heat-safe bowl, melt chocolate squares in microwave (approximately 30 seconds). Set aside. In a medium bowl, using an electric mixer on medium speed, beat the softened cream cheese and milk together until well blended. Gradually add in the sugar ½ a cup at a time, until well blended. Stir in melted chocolate, vanilla and salt. Fold in marshmallows.

2. Drop rounded tablespoon sized amounts of mixture into the shredded coconut and roll until well coated and place on plate. Repeat this step for remaining mixture. Cover and chill in refrigerator. Serve cold.

Cupcake Cones

THESE LITTLE TREATS ARE SURE TO DELIGHT EVERYONE. YOU CAN FILL THE CONE WITH almost anything, from candy to pudding or frosting, fruit, yogurt and even diamonds! Make these for parties or decorate them more conservatively and serve them at dinner parties or favors at weddings.

- 12 ice cream cones
- 1 container of white or chocolate frosting
- 1 package white or chocolate cake mix

- 1 cup assorted candies (your choice)
- ½ cup candy sprinkles (your choice)

1. Prepare the packaged cake mix following the directions on the box. Pour into a nonstick mini muffin tray and follow the baking time instructions on the package (for standard cake mixes a mini muffin tray will usually bake at 350°F for 20-22 minutes) A mini cup or tray is approximately 2-inches in diameter which is a perfect cake size for the ice cream cone.

2. Once you have baked the mini muffin cakes, set aside to cool, then remove from tin.

3. Fill the cone with candies, chocolates or whatever you desire. Place the baked mini muffin cake in the cone and decorate with frosting. Sprinkle the tops with candies and enjoy.

Cone Filling ideas
jelly beans, gum drops, candies, licorice, flavored yogurt, puddings, marshmallows, nuts, chopped fruit, peanut butter

Butter Tart Pie

MY MOM LOVES BUTTER TARTS, SO I MADE THIS RECIPE JUST FOR HER. LOVE YOU MOM

- **Pastry:**
- 1 ½ cups all-purpose flour
- ½ cup ground walnuts
- 2½ tablespoons brown sugar
- ½ teaspoon orange zest
- ½ teaspoon salt
- ¼ cup cold unsalted butter, cubed
- 1 egg yolk
- 2 tablespoons water

- **Tart Filling:**
- 1¼ cups brown sugar
- 2 teaspoons cornstarch
- 4 large eggs
- 1 cup corn syrup
- ¼ cup butter, softened
- 2 teaspoons vanilla
- 1½ cups walnuts, chopped

1. Preheat oven to 375°F.

2. To make pastry—In a large bowl, combine the flour, walnuts, brown sugar orange zest and salt. Using a pastry blender or two knives, cut in the butter until mixture resembles coarse crumbs. Whisk egg yolk with water and blend into flour mixture. Press dough firmly into an 8½-inch tart pan. Refrigerate for 30 minutes.

3. To make Filling—In a small bowl, combine the sugar with the cornstarch. In a large bowl, beat eggs until pale and fluffy. Beat in the sugar mixture, corn syrup, butter and vanilla. Sprinkle walnuts over the bottom of the pastry shell and pour filling evenly over top. Bake tart in oven for 55-60 minutes or until crust is golden and the filling is just firm to the touch.

Plum Crumble

Serves 4

PIES AND CRUMBLES ARE A COUPLE OF MY ALL-TIME FAVORITE DESSERTS TO MAKE AND EAT. They are quick and easy to put together and always taste great. Plum is my favorite, but peaches, apples, pears and cherries are amazing too.

- **Fruit Mixture:**
- **4 cups sliced plums**
- **½ cup sugar**
- **¼ cup all-purpose flour**
- **½ teaspoon cinnamon**

Topping:
- **⅓ cup all-purpose flour**
- **⅓ cup rolled oats**
- **⅓ cup brown sugar**
- **½ teaspoon cinnamon**
- **¼ cup unsalted butter**

1. Preheat oven to 375°F.

2. Filling—In a large bowl, combine the plums, sugar, ¼ cup flour and cinnamon, toss to mix. Transfer mixture to an 8-inch nonstick baking dish.

3. Topping—In a separate bowl, combine the ⅓ cup flour, oats, brown sugar and cinnamon. Using a pastry blender or two knives, cut in the butter until mixture resembles coarse crumbs. Sprinkle evenly over plums. Bake for 35-45 minutes or until golden brown. Serve warm with ice cream.

Pumpkin Cheesecake

AN ELEGANT AND EXTRA SPECIAL DESSERT FOR THE HOLIDAYS

- **Crust:**
- **1¼ cups graham wafer crumbs**
- **¼ cup sugar**
- **¼ cup unsalted butter, melted**
- **½ teaspoon cinnamon**
- **Filling:**
- **1 (14 oz.) canned pumpkin filling**

- **2 (8 oz.) packages cream cheese**
- **1½ cups whipping cream 35%**
- **¼ cup sugar**
- **2 large eggs**
- **1 teaspoon ground ginger**
- **1½ teaspoons pumpkin pie spice**

1. Preheat oven to 375°F.

2. Crust—in a large bowl, mix together all the ingredients for the crust. Press firmly onto the bottom and half way up the side of a 9 inch springform pan.

3. Filling—In a large bowl, using an electric mixer on medium speed, beat the pumpkin filling and cream cheese together until smooth. Stir in the whipping cream, sugar, eggs, ginger and pie spice until well blended.

4. Pour into a springform pan and bake for 30 minutes. Turn off the oven but leave the cake in the oven and let sit for 30 minutes. Remove from oven and refrigerate for at least 4 hours or overnight. Slice and top with whip cream. Enjoy.

Red Velvet Cupid Cakes

Makes 20 Mini Cakes

WHAT SAYS I LOVE YOU MORE THEN A RED VELVET HEART MINI CAKE? THESE CUTE LITTLE heart cakes filled with raspberry preserves, dusted with icing sugar will surely warm the hearts of your loved ones.

- 1½ cups all-purpose flour
- 1½ cups sugar
- 1 teaspoon baking soda
- 1 teaspoon salt
- 1 teaspoon cocoa powder
- 1½ cups vegetable oil
- 1 cup butter milk
- 2 large eggs

- 2 tablespoons red food coloring
- 1 teaspoon white distilled vinegar
- 1 teaspoon vanilla extract
- 1 cup raspberry preserves
- heart shaped cutters (large and small)

1. Preheat oven to 350°F.

2. In a medium bowl, sift together the flour, sugar, baking soda, salt and cocoa powder. In a larger bowl, using an electric mixer on medium speed, gently beat together the oil, buttermilk, eggs, food coloring, vinegar and vanilla. Add the flour mixture into the milk-egg mixture and mix until smooth and thoroughly combined (approximately 2 minutes).

3. Pour batter into a nonstick 13x9-inch cake pan and bake for 25-30 minutes or until a wooden toothpick comes out clean when inserted in the center. Let cake cool completely on rack. Transfer cake to flat surface and using the large heart-shaped cutter pressing firmly, stamp out heart-shaped cakes, until you have stamped out as many as possible. Using the smaller heart-shaped cutter, press into the center of the larger heart cakes (this will form the cavity for the filling). Remove the center from the cake you have just stamped using the smaller cutter and reserve for later use. Transfer the large heart cakes to serving plates and fill each cavity with the raspberry preserves. Place the reserved small heart cake beside the larger heart. Dust the whole plate with icing sugar and serve.

Sweet Love Cakes

Makes 12 Cupcakes

SWEET CUPCAKES WITH A CHOCOLATE GANACHE FROSTING.

- 12 tablespoons (1½ sticks) unsalted butter
- 1 cup sugar
- 4 large eggs, room temperature
- 1 (16 oz.) container chocolate syrup

- 2 tablespoons Ice wine
- 1 cup all-purpose flour
- ½ teaspoon salt
- ½ cup heavy cream
- 8 ounces semisweet chocolate chips

1. Preheat oven to 325°F.

2. In a large bowl using an electric mixer, beat the butter and sugar until light and fluffy. Add in the eggs, one at a time. Mix in the chocolate syrup and Ice wine. Add in the flour and the salt. Blend to combine ingredients only, be careful not to over mix.

3. Scoop the batter into prepared muffin cups and bake for 30 minutes or just until the middle has set. Allow to cool.

4. For the ganache—Using a double boiler (or a heat-safe bowl over a pot of simmering warm water), cook the cream and stir in the chocolate chips. Mix until smooth. Dip each cupcake into the ganache, covering the top. Place on rack to set. Do not place in refrigerator. Enjoy.

Easy Dreamy Fudge

THIS FUDGE RECIPE IS SO SIMPLE TO PREPARE. IT DOESN'T INVOLVE A CANDY THERMOMETER or tempering chocolate. This fudge is creamy and decadent. The perfect fix for any chocoholic or that late night sweet-tooth.

- **2 cups semisweet chocolate chips**
- **¾ cup milk chocolate chips**
- **1 can (14 oz.) sweetened condensed milk**
- **2 ounces unsweetened chocolate, coarsely chopped**
- **½ cup chopped walnuts (optional)**

1. Line a 9x5-inch square pan (or any size—8x8 or 9x3-inch—close to this) with foil or parchment paper and lightly grease.

2. Melt all the chocolates in a medium saucepan over low heat, stirring consistently. Remove from heat and stir in condensed milk (the mixture will begin to thicken). Add the walnuts, mix until blended.

3. Pour mixture into the bottom of the prepared dish and spread evenly. Refrigerate until firm (approximately 2-3 hours or overnight). Remove fudge from dish and place on cutting board. (I usually let the fudge sit at room temperature, just for a bit to soften a little before slicing. This makes it a little easier to cut and also safer—chilled fudge is very hard). Remove foil and cut into desired size squares. Enjoy.

Grilled Peaches with Honey and Mascarpone Serves 6

GRILLED PEACHES FILLED WITH MASCARPONE CHEESE, DRIZZLED WITH HONEY AND SPRINKLED with walnuts. A light but tasteful dessert. A great way to end any meal.

- **6 large ripe peaches, halved and pit removed**
- **6 tablespoons honey, plus extra for serving**
- **1 teaspoon cinnamon**

- **1 cup (8 oz.) mascarpone cheese, at room temperature**
- **¼ cup walnuts, chopped**

1. Preheat the oven to 375°F.

2. Heat a grill pan until hot and brush with a little oil, so the peaches won't stick. Place the peaches, cut side down, and grill for 2-3 minutes or until lightly charred.

3. Transfer the peaches to an oven-proof dish (cut side up) and drizzle the top of each peach with honey, followed by a sprinkle of cinnamon. Bake the peaches for 10 minutes or until very tender. Plate the peaches and serve with a dollop of mascarpone cheese over top and chopped walnuts. Drizzle with more honey if desired.

Peanut Butter Tiramisu

OKAY… YOU KNOW HOW MUCH I LOVE PEANUT BUTTER—BECAUSE I MENTION IT ALL THE time, and you're probably thinking—does she have to put it in everything? Well, I try to. Peanut butter tiramisu has all the creamy and satisfying comfort of a traditionally prepared tiramisu, but the peanut butter gives it that little added flavor and richness. Peanut butter, chocolate and coffee tiramisu… a good addition to follow my other guilty pleasure… a jar of extra-smooth peanut butter and a big spoon.

- **6 egg yolks, room temperature**
- **¼ cup sugar**
- **1½ cups mascarpone cheese**
- **¼ cup smooth peanut butter**
- **1½ cups espresso, cooled**
- **1 tablespoon Kahlúa**
- **1 package ladyfingers (approximately 24)**
- **½ cup semi-sweet chocolate shavings**

1. In a large bowl using an electric mixer, beat the egg yolks with the sugar until thick and pale (approximately 5 minutes). Add the mascarpone cheese and peanut butter and continue to beat until smooth. Add one tablespoon of the espresso and mix thoroughly, until all ingredients are combined.

2. In a shallow dish, combine the remaining espresso and the Kahlúa. Dip each ladyfinger into the espresso-Kahlúa for about 5 seconds or just enough to soak up some liquid (letting the ladyfingers soak too long will cause them to get mushy and fall apart). Place the soaked ladyfinger on the bottom of a deep dish (13x9-inches), breaking in half if needed to shape and fill in areas.

3. Spread evenly ½ of the mascarpone-peanut butter mixture over the ladyfingers. Arrange another layer of soaked ladyfingers over top and then finish by topping with the remaining mascarpone-peanut butter mixture. Cover the tiramisu with plastic wrap and refrigerate for at least 2 hours (up to 8 hours) to set. Remove from fridge and sprinkle the top with the chocolate shavings. Serve and enjoy.

Decadent Carrot Cake

I'VE TRIED LOTS OF DIFFERENT CARROT CAKES, BUT THIS RECIPE IS MY FAVORITE. I LIKE TO use raisins in the cake and pecans sprinkled over top, but feel free to exclude them if you choose.

- 2 cups all-purpose flour
- 2 teaspoons baking powder
- ½ teaspoon salt
- 2 teaspoons ground cinnamon
- ½ teaspoon allspice
- 1 cup (2 sticks) unsalted butter, melted
- 1½ cups sugar
- ½ cup brown sugar
- 4 large eggs
- ⅓ cup orange juice

- 4 cups grated carrots
- ½ cup raisins
- Frosting:
- 2 (8 oz.) packages cream cheese, room temperature
- ½ cup (1 stick) unsalted butter, room temperature
- 2 cups confectioner's sugar
- 1 teaspoon vanilla extract
- ½ cup chopped pecans

1. Preheat oven to 350°F.

2. In a medium bowl, combine the flour, baking powder, salt, cinnamon and allspice. In a large bowl and using an electric mixer on medium speed, beat the butter with the sugar and brown sugar until blended. Add in the eggs, one at a time, and beat well. Stir in the orange juice. Gradually beat the flour mixture into the butter-egg mixture. Stir in the carrots and raisins (raisins are optional). Pour batter into two 9-inch round nonstick baking pans and bake for 40 minutes or until cake pulls away from the sides of pan. Cool on rack and remove from pan.

3. For the frosting—Using an electric mixer, add all the ingredients except nuts, and beat until fluffy. Spread the frosting on top of each cake layer. Stack the cakes and sprinkle the top layer with the nuts (optional). Serve.

Index

Metric Measurement Conversion Chart

Fluid Measures

Fluid Ounces	U.S.	Milliliters
1/4	2 teaspoons	10
1/2	1 tablespoons	14
1	2 tablespoons	28
2	1/4 cup	56
4	1/2 cup	110
6	3/4 cup	170
8	1 cup	225
10	1 1/4 cups	280
12	1 1/2 cups	340
16	2 cups	450
18	2 1/4 cups	500,1/2 liter
20	2 1/2 cups	560
24	3 cups	675
27	3 1/2 cups	750
30	3 3/4 cups	840
32	4 cups / 1 quart	900
36	4 1/2 cups	1000, 1 liter
40	5 cups	1120

Solid Measures
U.S. and Imperial Measures

Ounces	Pounds	Metric Measures Grams	Kilos
1		28	
2		56	
3 1/2		100	
4	1/4	112	
5		140	
6		168	
8	1/2	225	
9		250	1/4
12	3/4	340	
16	1	450	
18		500	1/2
20	1 1/4	560	
24	1 1/2	675	
27		750	3/4
28	1 3/4	780	
32	2	900	
36	2 1/4	1000	1
40	2 1/2	1100	
48	3	1350	
54		1500	1 1/2

Oven Temperature Equivalent

Fahrenheit	Celsius	Description
225	110	Cool
250	130	
275	140	Very Slow
300	150	
325	170	Slow
350	180	Moderate
375	190	
400	200	Moderately Hot
425	220	Fairly Hot
450	230	Hot
475	240	Very Hot
500	250	Extremely Hot

Thank You

Thank you to everyone who has brought *Cooking Up Comfort* into their home—I hope you will use this book to bring fun and enjoyment into cooking, and create many tasty pleasures for yourself, family and friends. Thank you to my family and friends for your support and words of encouragement.

Mostly, thank you to my loving husband Peter, for always believing in me and giving me the opportunity in life to do what I love and enjoy... and for graciously eating dozens of test cookies without ever a complaint.

Thank you all again,

xoxo Althea